Inductive Reasoning in the Secondary Classroom

Gloria A. Neubert and James B. Binko

National Education Association
Washington, D.C.

ACKNOWLEDGMENTS

The authors wish to express their gratitude to the teachers who completed their national survey on inductive teaching, and to the many students who field tested parts of this text. Additionally, the following individuals granted interviews and/or did substantive reviews of the material: Penelope Booth, Elizabeth Bratton, Mary Cary, James Lawlor, Brooke Loudermilk, Loren Loudermilk, Sally McNelis, George Newberry, Janet Newberry, Allan Starkey, Lois Stover, and Leon Ukens.

Printing History
First Printing: February 1992

Note

The opinions expressed in this publication should not be construed as representing the policy or position of the National Education Association. Materials published by the NEA Professional Library are intended to be discussion documents for teachers who are concerned with specialized interests of the profession.

Library of Congress Cataloging-in-Publication Data

Neubert, Gloria A.
    Inductive reasoning in the secondary classroom / by Gloria A. Neubert and James B. Binko.
        p.   cm.—(NEA aspects of learning)
    Includes bibliographical references (p.).
    ISBN 0-8106-3010-9
    1. Logic in teaching.   2. Induction (Logic)—Study and teaching (Secondary) I. Binko, James B.   II. Title.   III. Series: Aspects of learning.
BC161.T4N48   1992
161'.071'273—dc20   90-25468

20

90-25468
CIP

CONTENTS

INTRODUCTION 7

CHAPTER 1. WHAT IS THE INDUCTIVE
APPROACH? 11
Readiness 11
Purpose for Reading 11
Summary 16
Identification/Analysis 17
Guided Practice 18

CHAPTER 2. WHY USE THE INDUCTIVE
APPROACH? 19
Readiness 19
Purpose for Reading 19
Empirical Research Findings 19
Arguments for the Inductive Approach . 20
Arguments Against the Inductive
Approach 26
Summary 29
Knowledge Check 30
Guided Practice 31

CHAPTER 3. HOW TO USE THE INDUCTIVE
APPROACH FOR CONCEPT
DEVELOPMENT 33
Readiness 33
Purpose for Reading 34
The Instructional Importance of
Concepts 35
Planning the Inductive Approach for
Concept Development 37
Summary 55

Knowledge Check 56
Guided Practice 56

CHAPTER 4. HOW TO USE THE INDUCTIVE
APPROACH FOR PRINCIPLE
FORMATION 57

Readiness 57
Purpose for Reading 57
Planning the Inductive Approach for
Principle Formation 59
Summary 71
Knowledge Check 72
Guided Practice 72

CHAPTER 5. INDUCTIVE REASONING IN
ENGLISH 73

Readiness 73
Purpose for Reading 73
Lesson 1. Prewriting Lesson for
Personality Profile Composition
(Grade 11) 74
Lesson 2. Language Minilesson on
Punctuating Dialogue (Grade 8) . . . 77
Identification/Analysis 81
Guided Practice 82

CHAPTER 6. INDUCTIVE REASONING IN
MATHEMATICS 85

Readiness 85
Purpose for Reading 86
Lesson 1. Pre-Algebra 86
Lesson 2. General Mathematics 90
Identification/Analysis 95
Guided Practice 98

CHAPTER 7. INDUCTIVE REASONING IN
            SCIENCE 101
    Readiness 101
    Purpose for Reading 102
        Lesson 1. Vertebrates and Their
            Characteristics (Grade 9) 103
        Lesson 2. Balancing (Grade 11) 106
    Identification/Analysis 109
    Guided Practice 110

CHAPTER 8. INDUCTIVE REASONING IN
            SOCIAL STUDIES 113
    Readiness 113
    Purpose for Reading 114
        Lesson 1. Characteristics of Citizenship
            (Grade 8) 114
        Lesson 2. Population Densities
            (Grade 11). 117
    Identification/Analysis 120
    Guided Practice. 121

Bibliography. 123

The Authors

Gloria A. Neubert is Professor and Director of the Teacher-Research Institute, College of Education, Towson State University.

James B. Binko is Dean, College of Education, Towson State University.

The Advisory Panel

Paul K. Adams, Professor of Educational and Intellectual History, Gannon University, Erie, Pennsylvania

Evelyn Beamer, English Teacher, Galax High School, Virginia

J. Merrell Hansen, Associate Professor, Department of Secondary Education, Brigham Young University, Provo, Utah

Wil S. Higuchi, Secondary Science Teacher, Sidney Public Schools, Nebraska

James E. Krolikowski, Social Studies Teacher, Manchester Memorial High School, New Hampshire

Eula Ewing Monroe, Professor, Teacher Education, Western Kentucky University, Bowling Green

Claire E. Ritterhoff, Reading Specialist, Randallstown High School, Baltimore County Public Schools, Maryland

Louise Sterett, Mathematics Teacher, Lyons Township High School, La Grange, Illinois

INTRODUCTION

Much public attention has been focused on the alleged failure of American students to master basic skills in reading, writing, arithmetic, and science, but a more disturbing finding shows that few can use their knowledge effectively in thinking and reasoning. In their report on a 20-year project mandated by Congress, officials of the National Assessment of Educational Progress (NAEP) (24)* observe that students have, in fact, made some improvement in the four core subjects, but that schools must now move beyond teaching basics so that their graduates can perform well in an increasingly complex world.

The NAEP report, *Crossroads in American Education*, is based on tests of 1.4 million students—ages 9, 13, and 17—in the four core subjects. Its findings constantly emphasize the need to do more with reasoning abilities in the classroom. For instance, according to the investigation, only 39 percent of 17-year-olds can find, understand, summarize, and explain information about the subjects they study. The report concludes that American students are seriously lacking in higher-order thinking, and it urges teachers to use approaches that will require them to move away from their traditional authoritarian roles as the primary source of knowledge. Instead, lessons should require students to take a more active and responsible role in learning rather than being passive recipients of someone else's discoveries.

This study gives credence to recommendations by other educational groups, including the learned societies in English, mathematics, science, and social studies, urging teachers to give more attention to student abilities in analyzing, classifying, comparing, formulating hypotheses, and drawing conclusions—i.e., thinking skills essential to reasoning processes.

---

*Numbers in parentheses appearing in the text refer to the Bibliography beginning on page 123.

The purpose of this text is to teach you one model of instruction for developing students' reasoning abilities while teaching the content of your discipline. Specifically, this text is designed to give you practical and theoretically sound assistance in learning how to use the inductive approach, a teaching approach that actively involves students in the use of their own reasoning while learning the content of your discipline.

Unlike many other texts written about pedagogy, this text is not intended to simply *transmit* knowledge about the inductive approach. It is designed to involve you actively, so that you will construct knowledge as you read, and ultimately be able to write inductive lessons for your secondary students.

In order to facilitate this process, each chapter begins with Readiness, a section that asks you to recall experience pertinent to what you are about to learn. Its purpose is to mobilize your background so that you can relate the new information to what you already know—a necessary step if new information is to be meaningful to you, the learner and teacher.

Next is Purpose for Reading, a set of questions to answer while you read. These questions will help you focus attention on the information in the chapter and will keep you actively involved processing the information as you search for answers.

At the end of the chapters, you will find a series of activities designed to lead you through the developmental steps of the learning process. Knowledge Check asks you to tell what you have learned about the approach or about its supporting theory and research. Identification/Analysis involves you in analyzing specific examples of the approach. Finally, Guided Practice gives you opportunities to design components of, and eventually complete, inductive lessons for your own discipline. Often these activities encourage you to interact with a partner—another student in your workshop or a colleague in your school—in order to facilitate and affirm your learning.

Chapters 1 to 4 are generic in nature. They are meant to be read by secondary teachers regardless of the academic content they teach—English, mathematics, social studies, science. Chapter 1 identifies the concept of inductive reasoning, differentiates between expository and inductive teaching, and provides classroom examples of both approaches. With these concrete classroom examples firmly established, you will be ready to comprehend Chapter 2, which presents a rationale for inductive reasoning in the classroom, including arguments for and against. The chapter also includes a succinct review of research and theory associated with induction, testimony by classroom teachers, and a summary case for including inductive reasoning as a regular and systematic feature of classroom activity. Chapters 3 and 4 explicate the inductive approach as it relates to the teaching of concepts and principles, respectively; these chapters offer specific guidelines to help you develop each step of the inductive approach. Note, too, that these first four chapters contain several opportunities to use inductive reasoning to learn the inductive approach—that is, we have used the inductive approach to teach you how to teach inductively.

The remaining four chapters deal specifically with subject matter disciplines—English, mathematics, science, and social studies. They are designed to give you information and necessary focused practice in using induction within your field. Each chapter concludes with examples and instruction for writing inductive lessons for the particular discipline. Before drafting your inductive lessons for Guided Practice, however, we recommend that you skim the lesson descriptions and explications in the other three discipline chapters to gather even more ideas for writing interesting and effective inductive lessons for your subject. For example, Chapter 6, "Inductive Reasoning in Mathematics," contains a lesson that demonstrates how to introduce new content-specific terminology for the language students use in their generalization; Chapter 8, "Inductive Reasoning in Social Studies," provides a lesson on being a "good citizen," a concept that does not have one absolute set of essential attributes.

9

This text includes many specific examples of lessons taught inductively to help you understand how to plan and implement the specifics of this approach in a secondary setting. In 1989 we conducted a national survey of English, mathematics, science, and social studies teachers and asked them to contribute inductive lessons they had used successfully. It is our hope that the examples, our narrative, and the developmental activities will allow you to take the essence of this text—the framework of the inductive approach—shape it carefully to fit the fabric of your own unique teaching style, and make it an active part of your teaching repertoire.

It is not our intention to advertise the inductive approach as the only teaching approach that should be used in the academic disciplines. That would be inappropriate and unrealistic. As the text will reveal, however, there is evidence that students' use of inductive reasoning—a thinking skill, central to academic success, thoughtful citizenship, and career mobility—is being neglected within the secondary classroom. The time has come to reverse that trend.

Chapter 1

WHAT IS THE INDUCTIVE APPROACH?

READINESS

Teachers have different teaching styles. Some use small group discussion; some lecture; some ask questions of the entire class. Some use predominantly one approach; others combine approaches.

Recall two teachers you had as a student whose teaching styles differed. They could have been your elementary, high school, or college teachers. How did they typically conduct their classes? What made their teaching styles different? Did you prefer one style over another?

PURPOSE FOR READING

Read the following three lesson descriptions. All deal with the same content, but each one uses a different approach. As you read, note (1) the goal of each lesson and (2) how each lesson differs from the other two with respect to the role of the teacher and the role of the student.

LESSON 1. Ms. Adams begins the class by telling the eighth graders that today they will continue their unit Greek Myths and Legends. They will discuss two stories that they read for homework, the myths of Theseus and Perseus. The teacher proceeds to explain that Theseus and Perseus are classical heroes because they possess the following attributes: superhuman powers; often had a parent who was a god, goddess, or was of noble birth; the ability to accept challenges and perform miraculous feats; and a destructive human frailty. She then points out specific examples of these attributes in the two assigned readings. For example, Ms. Adams refers students to the pages in the text that describe how Theseus performed the miraculous feats of capturing the bull of Marathon and slaying the minotaur and how Perseus killed Medusa. She encourages students to take notes during her explanation. For homework, she instructs the class to read another myth, the myth of Jason, in order to determine if he also possesses the attributes of the classical hero.

LESSON 2. Mr. Barnes begins his lesson by telling his students that they will continue their unit Greek Myths and Legends, and today they will focus on the myths of Theseus and Perseus. He explains that Theseus and Perseus are classical heroes because they demonstrate certain attributes: superhuman powers; often had a parent who was a god or goddess, or was of noble birth; an ability to accept challenges and perform miraculous feats; and a destructive human frailty. He then directs his students to work in assigned pairs and find examples of these attributes in the stories of Theseus and Perseus. After a few minutes of student collaboration, Mr. Barnes leads a consensus discussion asking students to provide examples for each attribute in both myths. For homework, he assigns the class a third reading, the myth of Jason, in order to determine if Jason possesses the attributes of a classical hero.

LESSON 3. Mrs. Carter begins by telling students they will continue their study of Greek myths and legends. She had previously instructed them to read the myths of Theseus and Perseus, and to complete a chart about the two central characters (see Figure 1.1).

Mrs. Carter instructs her students to work in pairs, to compare their findings, and to make a list of the similarities they find between the characters of Theseus and Perseus. After her students have had a few minutes to collaborate, Mrs. Carter leads an entire-class discussion to reach consensus on these similarities. If necessary, she is prepared to use additional eliciting questions, such as "Who were Theseus's parents?" "Perseus's parents?" "What, therefore, did these two characters have in common?"

"Was Theseus perfect?" "What did he do that revealed his weakness?" "Was Perseus perfect?" "How did he reveal his weakness?" "What, therefore, do these heroes have in common?" At the end of the exercise when the list of similarities is complete, the teacher reveals that these similarities are attributes of "classical heroes," attributes that all Greek heroes share. For homework, she instructs students to read another myth, the myth about Jason, to determine if he is a classical hero.

These three lessons have the same goal: to teach students the attributes of a "classical hero." But each teacher approaches the task differently.

The approach in Lesson 1 is *expository—the teacher, Ms. Adams, states the generalization.* She is the explainer. She presents the content to learners "in final form" (4, p. 16). She decides during her planning how to sequence and pace the information for students. It is also her responsibility to present the information in language understandable to her students. It is she

Figure 1.1

	THESEUS	PERSEUS
Parents		
Tests/Feats		
Abilities		
Weaknesses		

who decides whether to present the information through inductive or deductive reasoning (see Figure 1.2). In an *inductive* presentation, the teacher gives specific facts or examples, then follows by stating the generalization derived from these facts or examples. In a *deductive* presentation, the teacher states the generalization first, then follows with specific facts or examples to support that generalization.

Ms. Adams's lesson was presented deductively, since she first gave students the generalization—attributes of the classical hero. Then she proceeded to give specific examples of each attribute from the two stories. In this type of lesson, the students are listeners. No independent discovery is required of them. It is their responsibility to be attentive in order to learn the information the teacher tells them, but there is no guarantee they are engaged in reasoning themselves, since the generalizations and examples are presented and explained to them by the teacher.

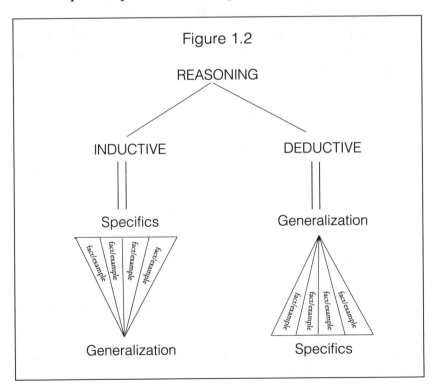

Figure 1.2

REASONING

INDUCTIVE   DEDUCTIVE

Specifics   Generalization

Generalization   Specifics

The lesson is, in fact, a better and more explicit demonstration of the *teacher's* reasoning abilities than the students'.

The approach in Lesson 2 is also expository. The teacher gives students the generalization he wants—the attributes of a classical hero. The content, as in the first lesson, is presented deductively: the teacher begins with the generalization, then follows with a class discussion in which students are asked to identify specific examples to support the generalization. This lesson differs from the first only in that it is more student-centered; that is, instead of the teacher explicating the examples of the heroic attributes, the students themselves locate and explain the examples. Because students are searching the stories for specifics, then explaining their examples during a class discussion, there is observable evidence that they, along with the teacher, are involved in deductive reasoning. However, the lesson is still expository since students get no experience in making generalizations.

The teacher's approach in Lesson 3 is an example of *guided inductive discovery.* In discovery learning, the teacher does not give students "the principal content of what is to be learned" (4, p. 16). The key concept or principle—the generalization—"is not explicitly communicated . . . to the learner" (84, p. 45). The learner is expected to complete the learning task with little or no help from the teacher. If the teacher provides considerable help, as in this lesson with the structured chart and eliciting questions, the instruction is termed *guided discovery.* The purpose of this guidance is to reduce distracting errors and the time necessary for discovering the generalization.

This guided discovery lesson is planned and conducted inductively. Mrs. Carter uses a series of *eliciting questions,* questions designed to guide students toward the statement of the generalization. First, she instructs her students to read the two myths, to record the specifics on a chart, and then to note the similarities between the two characters. Through class discussion, and aided by the chart, she uses additional eliciting questions about the heroes' parents, weaknesses, etc., to help students infer the four attributes that characterize a classical hero, a label that Mrs. Carter provides at the end of the inductive exercise. *Thus, the teacher guides students to reason inductively, that is, to examine an appropriate number of specifics, in some prescribed order, notice similarities, and then infer a generalization.* The validity of the generalization, and how well students understand it, are then tested through an activity that requires students to apply the generalization to a new set of specifics. In the case of the generalization about attributes of classical heroes, the activity is to apply the list to a third myth, Jason.

Also notice that this lesson has a greater degree of active student involvement than Lessons 1 and 2. The students are actively engaged in both finding specifics and producing the generalization; that is, they are engaged in inductive reasoning. In Lessons 1 and 2 the teachers perform the inductive reasoning and give the generalizations to students.

SUMMARY

In an *expository* lesson, the teacher performs the reasoning, and states the generalization of the lesson. The students may or may not be involved in the explication of the specifics to support the generalization.

In a guided inductive discovery lesson, hereafter called the *inductive approach*, the students, not the teacher, state the generalization following their examination of specifics. In order to establish the background for making the generalization, the following pattern is employed by the teacher:

1. Students examine specifics (facts/examples) selected by the teacher.
2. Students answer the teacher's eliciting questions.
3. Students infer the generalization.
4. Students apply the generalization(s) to new specifics.

16

IDENTIFICATION/ANALYSIS

1. Examine the following lesson description.
   What specifics are examined?
   What is the generalization?
   Who states the generalization? Therefore, does this lesson employ the inductive approach? Explain.
   What is the application activity?

Lesson Description 1. The mathematics teacher reviews with students what a triangle is, what an interior angle is, and how angles are measured. The teacher gives students pieces of construction paper and tells them to cut out three triangles of different sizes (small, medium, and large). Then they are to label the interior angles of each triangle *(a, b, c)*, to measure each angle with a protractor, and to record their measurements on the chart handed to them (see Figure 1.3).

After the measurements are complete, the teacher instructs students to add the measurements of each triangle. After each student reports to the entire class his/her sums for the small, medium and large triangles, the teacher asks, "What, then, can we conclude about the interior angles of any size triangle?" The appropriate student generalization is: "The sum of the interior

Figure 1.3

| | | ANGLE | | |
	a	b	c	SUM
TRIANGLE				
small				
medium				
large				

angles of any size triangle will always equal 180 degrees." (Teachers should be prepared to encounter some student measurements that do not add up to 180 degrees due to protractor interpretation error.)

Tomorrow, the teacher will introduce the principle of the sum of supplementary angles, and students will need to apply this principle of the sum of the interior angles in order to discover that the sum of supplementary angles is also 180 degrees.

    2. Examine the following lesson description.
       What specifics are examined?
       What are the generalizations?
       Who states the generalization? Therefore, does this lesson employ the inductive approach? Explain.
       What application activity is planned?

Lesson Description 2. The teacher displays three pictures: Washington, Lincoln, and Theodore Roosevelt. She asks students to make a list of the attributes for which each president is famous. (For example, Washington, our first president, for putting democracy into action; Lincoln for the Emancipation Proclamation; Roosevelt for the Panama Canal.) After students have had adequate time to prepare their lists, the teacher has them give their responses as she makes a master list on the board. When the lists are complete, the teacher points out the similarities among the three lists—each is considered a "great" president because each charted a new course for America. The teacher then tells students that they will view a film about John F. Kennedy. Their purpose for viewing is to use these attributes to determine if JFK was a "great" president.

GUIDED PRACTICE

Using the lesson pattern in the Summary on pages 16 and 17, transform Lesson 2 into the inductive approach. Verify your changes with a colleague.

Chapter 2

WHY USE THE INDUCTIVE APPROACH?

READINESS

Return to Mrs. Carter's lesson in Chapter 1. Imagine yourself as a student in her class. Make a list of advantages to you because of her use of the inductive approach. Also identify limitations to this approach.

PURPOSE FOR READING

1. What arguments are offered for using the inductive approach?
2. What arguments are offered against using the inductive approach? What rebuttals are given to the arguments?

Empirical Research Findings

The controversy over whether exposition or discovery is a more effective teaching approach, or whether induction or deduction is a better sequence, has been the focus of many empirical studies (for example, 1, 5, 8, 12, 28, 40, 41, 42, 43, 49, 51, 73, 86, 87). Findings from these studies are often inconclusive: generalizations about the use of these approaches in the classroom cannot be made with a great degree of certainty because of the conflicting definition of terms and crucial differences in study design. Additionally, some studies conducted under laboratory-type circumstances rather than in regular classrooms lack credibility with teachers. Some studies are one-shot attempts, conducted with programmed instruction or by someone other than a regular classroom teacher; others have inadequately described instructional procedures. Few studies have been in disciplines other than mathematics and science. Despite absence of absolute agreement among empirical studies, however, evidence does support the inductive approach—where students state the generalization—for promoting greater achievement, better transfer, and more student involvement and interest.

Arguments for the Inductive Approach

Many theorists argue that the inductive approach is highly effective as an instructional approach; many teachers testify that they find it to be a very successful approach for teaching content in the secondary school. The arguments they offer can be grouped into two categories: (1) the advantages of engaging students in thinking processes associated with inductive reasoning, and (2) the advantages of the student-centeredness inherent in the inductive approach.

Advantages of Inductive Reasoning

Through the inductive approach, three goals for the student can be pursued: (1) learning the content of the discipline, (2) practicing reasoning skills, and (3) developing confidence in reasoning ability. The expository approach emphasizes only the first of these goals, i.e., the acquisition of knowledge. Students are passive recipients of generalizations that have been discovered and put into words by someone else—the teacher, textbook authors, writers of the filmstrip, etc. Students become reproducers, not producers. This does not mean that they only memorize information under this approach—although that is a danger. They may indeed understand it, but they have no practice with the reasoning behind it. Exposition does not require students to use inductive reasoning, only to follow it. As Bruner observes in *Toward a Theory of Instruction*, we "teach a subject not to produce little living libraries on that subject, but rather to get a student to think mathematically for himself, to consider matters

20

as a historian does, to take part in the process of knowledge-getting" (15, p. 72). One high school teacher summarized by saying,

> I believe that our role as teachers is to make students think. Inductive techniques are a way to achieve independent thinking so students are not just parroting back information to us. That is not education.

In this world of ever-increasing knowledge, reflected in gargantuan curricula that teachers lament can never be "covered" adequately in the course of the school year, we must give students lifelong strategies for thinking systematically and independently. But a "majority of teachers do not regularly employ methods that encourage and develop thinking in their students" (59, p. 2). In far too many secondary classrooms today, the only people getting practice in inductive reasoning are the teachers. The teacher makes the meaning; the students take the meaning. The students become other-reliant, instead of self-reliant (67).

The more practice one has in reasoning, the more readily this essential cognitive process has a chance to transfer to life. As Kreiger (52) reminds us, in life, when a person reads a novel, no teacher is present to state the generalizations about the theme or the influential nature of particular characters. The reader must begin with page one, pick up cues along the way, and arrive at his or her own conclusions. The same can be said about arriving at pragmatic generalizations about political parties, and voting decisions based on these generalizations. Such are the reasoning skills that free us from what Smith (77) calls "soft-core ignorance"—reliance on others to tell us what to do; such are the reasoning skills necessary for critical thinking and problem solving; such are the reasoning skills necessary to become lifelong learners; such are the thinking processes of independent adults. And they cannot be "acquired by absorbing someone else's thought products" (47, p. 49).

By depriving students of opportunities to do inductive

reasoning, we also deny them the excitement and joy of discovery and the resulting confidence in their ability to think independently. Sorting through facts and discovering a generalization from them can be motivating. There is evidence that secondary students generally prefer the inductive approach to expository methods (70). One high school student, after a semester of British Writers taught inductively, described it this way, "I finally realized I wasn't stupid!" "A pretty scathing indictment of 12 years of teachers' lecturing at her!" commented her teacher.

The inductive approach also appeals to the personality and learning styles of those students who resist or are stifled by expository teaching. Students who find it difficult to accept the teacher or the textbook as the ultimate source of ideas find the inductive approach a comfortable classroom alternative (48). On the other hand, students who find it more comfortable to comply with the ideas of the teacher (l) are provided appropriate independent thinking opportunities through the inductive approach. One high school teacher reported that by encouraging inductive reasoning she is teaching students "that they have within *them* the ability to unlock new concepts and generalizations."

Student-Centeredness Inherent in the Inductive Approach

In *A Place Called School,* Goodlad reported on his in-depth study of 1,016 classrooms in America. He concludes that the major pedagogy in this country is teacher-centered/expository instruction, with the teacher "out-talking" the students three to one, and with students listening to the teacher or working alone on seatwork. Goodlad laments that he and his team saw little opportunity for students to develop their reasoning: "They scarcely ever speculated on meanings . . ." (35, p. 468). This criticism is echoed in most of the recent educational reports (11, 66, 76, 78).

Such a state of affairs in our nation's schools is incongruent with studies that indicate that "the more active involvement required of the organism, the greater the likelihood of learning" (48, p. 158; 88). Learning does not occur by passive absorption alone (71). When learners are actively engaged, their attention is maximized, and attention is a prerequisite for learning. With attention, some learning is certain to occur. Involvement also requires effort on the part of the student, and when one has to exert effort for anything, more value is attached to it (48).

Let's look again at the steps in the inductive approach:

1. Students examine specifics (cues/prompts) selected by the teacher.
2. Students answer the teacher's eliciting questions.
3. Students infer the generalization.
4. Students apply the generalization to new specifics.

Notice the subjects and the active verbs in the inductive pattern: "Students examine . . . answer . . . infer . . . apply." The students are *doing*, not just *hearing about*. They are actively engaged in the learning process and they must exert effort to learn. And because they have been so intimately involved in the creation of concepts and principles, they are better prepared to apply the generalization to new circumstances (67).

The inductive approach encourages student involvement; it should not, however, be assumed that this approach is one of pure or random discovery. That is, it is not an approach in which the teacher provides no guidance or direction, or one in which students are left to discover generalizations via trial and error. On the contrary, the inductive approach, used effectively, is a form of guided discovery. Studies have revealed that "the more guidance a learner receives, the more efficient his discovery will be; the more efficient discovery is, the more learning and transfer will occur" (22, p. 72). Teacher guidance reduces the search time required of students to discover the generalization; it speeds up the learning time; and it helps eliminate extreme or incorrect generalizations (32). Consequently, in the inductive approach, teachers use examples and eliciting questions (cues and prompts) generously, but it is the students who perform the reasoning and make the generalizations.

The teacher-directed aspect of the inductive approach is congruent with the work of Vygotsky who observed that students go through a period of proximal development—that is, a time when they can function "under adult guidance or in collaboration with more capable peers," but cannot function independently (83, p. 86). "What a child can do with assistance today she will be able to do by herself tomorrow" (83, p. 87). Thus the skillful teacher using the inductive approach provides adequate prompts and cues as a kind of intellectual scaffold for students, thereby nurturing in a disciplined and systematic manner their ability to reason independently.

An important component of this scaffolding is the opportunity for peer interaction during the inductive lesson. Recall the portion of Mrs. Carter's lesson in which she paired students to verify the independent work they had done on their charts, and then to collaborate on making a list of similarities between two heroes. The students participated in *collaborative learning*, a very effective form of "indirect teaching in which the teacher sets the problem and organizes students to work it out collaboratively" (14, p. 637). (It should be noted that Mrs. Carter could have used an entire-class discussion for this part of the lesson, but collaborative learning guarantees that more students will engage in the inductive reasoning because of the greater demands put on each person when there are fewer to participate in solving the problem.) Collaborative learning allows students to learn by talking the problem out with others.

Talking appears to be essential to the effectiveness of this strategy. Our brains think better with words. In fact, our brains are so word-dependent that "most people think only about things for which they have words and . . . only in the directions for which they have words" (54, p. 131). It has been shown that young children solve problems with the help of their own speech.

24

It is the unity of using what they perceive in the world, their speech and their actions, that allows them to solve the problems. In fact, the more complex the problem, the greater the role of speech for young children (83). Studies with secondary students have also revealed that talking facilitates the discovery of generalizations (34).

When used as an integral part of the inductive approach, collaborative learning requires students to interact with members of their group—to express their ideas orally. Some significant phenomena occur that reveal the essential role language plays in shaping a generalization. For example, a student may express an idea and then, immediately upon "hearing" it aloud, reject it as invalid. ("Oh no, that's not right!") Often students think their ideas are sound until they hear them in another "voice"—their spoken voice, rather than their mind's voice. Speech allows students to evaluate their thoughts.

Sometimes, of course, students erroneously or prematurely reject their own valid ideas. With the collaborative approach, the audience of peers is there to recognize and defend the validity of the idea, or take it up and modify it. In either case, the speaker's thinking has been shaped as a result of interacting with an audience of peers and the feedback inherent in the collaborative process.

Talking is also vital to our efforts to reshape our ideas. Sometimes students use talk to help them "think aloud," to monitor their thinking, to find out what they know, to discover connections, to reinterpret their perceived worlds. They talk, stop, start, stammer, rephrase, and use unfinished thoughts in an effort to discover. Talking is a vital part of reshaping ideas. Barnes (6, p. 28) calls this oral groping toward a meaning "exploratory talk," and sees it as an essential prerequisite if assimilation and accommodation of new knowledge into prior knowledge are to occur.

Another phenomenon that often occurs is the inability of students to express to their peers ideas that they were sure they understood as they thought about them. Consider this proposition: If we understand an idea, we can put it into words; if we do not understand it, coherent and relevant oral expression is impossible. Students who say "I understand it. I just can't explain it" probably do not understand. Sometimes knowing that one does not know is necessary motivation for attending to a group's discussion, picking up on the group's line of reasoning, and eventually participating in the formulation of the generalization.

When students are able to express their ideas within a group of peers, group members have an opportunity to react to the idea—to validate it, to extend it, to modify it, to support it, or to reject it. This is one further example of the influence peers may exert on one another as they reveal their thinking and move toward a generalization.

In the inductive approach, the resulting generalization is expressed in the students' language, and there is a greater probability they will both understand and remember it. Through discussion, students make sense of—organize—the specifics and develop a generalization. (They make it part of their linguistic networks and organize the new information as part of their cognitive structures.) Consequently, the information is stored in memory and readily available for future application.

When, however, a generalization is not discovered by students, but given to them by the teacher through expository teaching, the generalization is in someone else's words, and there is the danger it may not fit the students' linguistic network or cognitive structure. If this assimilation does not occur, the result is rote learning; students may be able to parrot back the generalization, but be unable to apply it in similar but new situations (e.g., in the homework assignment to read the Jason story to decide whether he is a classical hero), because they do not understand it.

Arguments Against the Inductive Approach

Few teachers argue that the inductive approach is

26

inappropriate for use in the secondary school. Those who voice skepticism usually cite time constraints and complications with using this approach with certain types of students.

The following comments from two secondary teachers reflect the frustrations with time: ⨯

> Time is the key factor. When I feel I have the time, I use inductive techniques. When the ever-increasing curriculum is accompanied by ever-increasing interruptions in instructional time, I tend to fall back on traditional lectures (exposition) to cover a lot of material quickly.
>
> Inductive teaching on a regular basis is very time-consuming. It's wonderful, but also hard to commit yourself to this fully when both the calendar and your supervisor keep reminding you that you still have half the book to cover.

Unfortunately, massive curricula have led teachers to accept this "covering" approach to instruction and they rely on "exposing" students to concepts and principles via an expository approach. What often results is the superficial "coverage" of content and the reduction or elimination of student opportunities to engage in reasoning in the classroom. It is an approach to teaching and a trend in schooling that discourages, rather than encourages, the kind of learning a real education is about.

Thinking takes time; teaching so that students understand and can apply learning to new situations takes time. And it is this commodity, time, that teachers single out as the most important deterrent to using the inductive approach. That is, there is not enough classroom time, some argue, to engage students inductively and still cover the content of the course.

Two perspectives may be useful in confronting the issue of time. First, there is never enough time, regardless of the methods teachers use, to cover everything. That reality is the answer, not the problem in instruction. Teachers who believe they can confidently cover everything in the course of study by simply using this or that approach have a terribly simple and restricted

27

view of their discipline. A second and useful perspective is this: The hours on the clock may be absolute, but *time* is relative. In learning, the value of time is relative to the outcomes of its use. Experience has demonstrated that when the inductive approach is planned properly—that is, when the teacher selects appropriate examples and asks strategic, eliciting questions for the discovery of generalizations—the inductive approach is an efficient one, especially considering the learning and transfer that result. As one teacher said, "Yes, the inductive approach takes a little more time, but it is definitely worth it, considering that the students remember the important concepts better." The classroom teacher, therefore, is advised to decide which concepts and principles are central to the lesson, unit, or course of study, and to use the inductive approach when introducing them.

Some teachers also voice concern about using the inductive approach with certain types of students:

> My sixth grade English classes are basic students, so I seldom use the inductive approach.

> I teach seventh grade general math and pre-algebra. Most of these 12-year-olds are not developmentally ready for inductive learning.

But other teachers report success in encouraging inductive reasoning with similar students:

> Children must start having regular practice with inductive reasoning at an early age. My fifth graders were mute when I started this, but at the end of the year were comfortably thinking inductively.

> I've been teaching for 12 years, secondary social studies to all ability levels, and have always used the inductive approach in my instruction. Currently I'm working with "at-risk" students, beginning with age 14, and find that once they have practice in the inductive method of learning, they find it more enjoyable than traditional expository approaches."

Low-achieving students are often initially reluctant and/or unprepared to take part in such an active learning experience (56). In fact, many types of students initially find the inductive approach problematic since most of them "have made a career of passive learning. When met by instructional situations in which they may have to use some mental energies, some students resist that intellectual effort" (81, p. 2). But practitioners and researchers have found that inductive reasoning is possible with all ages, abilities, and grade levels (26, 47, 80). Our experience with secondary students has convinced us that if teachers select appropriate concepts and principles to be learned, provide specific examples appropriate to students' backgrounds, and ask appropriate eliciting questions, secondary students, regardless of grade or ability, can learn by the inductive approach.

SUMMARY

There is considerable support for including inductive reasoning as a regular and central aspect of classroom activity. Although no single empirical study has demonstrated conclusively the superiority of inductive teaching to all other methods, overall evidence from research, theory, and practice clearly supports the approach. Recent studies of American secondary student performance show the need to emphasize teaching strategies that reward sound reasoning along with correct answers.

The landscape of inductive reasoning includes two features that classroom teachers intuitively recognize as both desirable and productive: a high level of student involvement and learning that results from student reasoning—not the teacher's. These twin features increase the probability that students will both understand and remember what they study inductively.

We have made the case that inductive reasoning is neither a random nor laissez-faire pedagogical enterprise. As teacher, you play a direct and essential role in structuring the classroom environment so that your students' learning is effective, time-efficient, and relevant to course content. The key to success for you and your students is your thoughtful and deliberate use of examples and questions to motivate and guide their reasoning.

The positive results for students engaged in inductive reasoning appear to outweigh any reported limitation. As a general rule, we recommend that you use the inductive approach when introducing concepts or principles that are fundamental to your students' understanding of a topic.

Just because we are recommending the use of the inductive approach for fundamental concepts and principles does not mean, however, that we are advocating the elimination of deductive reasoning (that is, having students support a generalization that the teacher presents) from secondary pedagogy. (For example, see Lesson 2 in Chapter 1.) Secondary teachers testify that when students have the background necessary to understand the teacher-stated generalization and the willingness to assimilate the generalization, the deductive approach can result in student learning. If the deductive approach is used exclusively, however, students are denied opportunities to arrive at generalizations—to construct their own knowledge. The thinking skill of inductive reasoning is too central to life to neglect nurturing in the classroom. And considering the transfer effects and attitudinal implications of the use of the inductive approach, secondary schools have a responsibility to put inductive reasoning into proper perspective among their teaching approaches.

KNOWLEDGE CHECK

Assume that your supervisor has just observed you teaching a lesson that involved students in inductive reasoning. You are very pleased with the results of the lesson, but your supervisor begins the debriefing with this question, "Why did you choose to use an inductive approach to achieve your content goals instead of an expository approach?" You are not sure whether she is just testing your ability to justify your choice or she believes you made the incorrect choice. Make a list of reasons you would give her.

GUIDED PRACTICE

Go back to page 17, Lesson Description 1. Where are the collaborative opportunities for students in this lesson? Briefly write how you would incorporate collaborative learning into this lesson in at least two places. Then share your ideas with a partner.

Chapter 3

HOW TO USE THE INDUCTIVE APPROACH FOR CONCEPT DEVELOPMENT

READINESS

Examine the two lists that follow. All the items in List A are labels for *concepts*. None of the statements in List B is a *concept*. What do the items in List A have in common with each other? How are List A and List B different, other than the fact that List A consists of single words or words with a modifier, and List B consists of statements? What is a *concept*?

List A–Concepts

verb	prime number
number	insect
subject	refraction
absolute location	freedom
metamorphosis	pitch
polygon	blind
revolution	suffer

List B

—A verb should be the same number as its subject.

—Native American Indians have suffered from concentration policies and broken treaties.

—The sum of the interior angles of a convex polygon of n sides is 180(n–2).

—Many common chemical compounds look dry but do contain water.

33

—Insects exhibiting complete metamorphosis do not compete for food.

—Hawthorne was pessimistic about the nature of humankind.

—Effective descriptive writing "shows" the reader instead of "telling" the reader.

—American and British revolutions produced lasting democracies; French and Latin American revolutions did not.

—Addition of any n can be undone by the subtraction of n and vice versa.

PURPOSE FOR READING

1. What is a *concept?* After reading this chapter, compare your answer from the Readiness section.
2. Why are *concepts* important to disciplines?
3. What are the steps in an inductive approach to concept development?

A *concept* is a set of objects, conditions, events, or processes that can be grouped together based on common characteristics they share (63, 82). For example, the figures shown in Figure 3.1

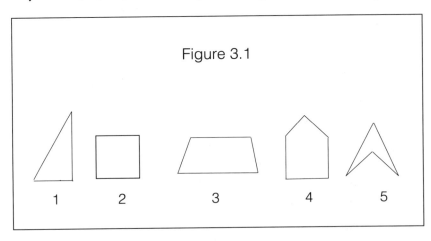

Figure 3.1

are all *polygons*—concrete objects that can be grouped together because they share the common characteristics of being closed plane figures bounded by straight lines.

Some concepts are quite concrete in that their common characteristics, called "essential attributes," are all observable (e.g., the concept *insect* has the common characteristics of a head, thorax, abdomen, legs, and wings, all of which can be seen). Other concepts are abstract in that few if any of their essential attributes can be observed (e.g., *freedom*, and *number* in the grammatical sense).

Concepts are usually symbolized by a single word (e.g., *verb, refraction*) or a word plus a few modifiers (e.g., *absolute location, prime number*). This word is the concept label; the statement that specifies all the essential attributes of a concept is the *generalization*. The following are generalizations for some of the concepts in List A. Notice that each specifies all the essential attributes of the concept. The concept label appears in parenthesis.

- Any part of speech that denotes action or state of being. *(verb)*
- Any location of a region in reference to the earth's grid system and to recording its latitude and longitude. *(absolute location)*
- Any developmental process common to insects and amphibians characterized by an abrupt, hormonally induced and regulated transformation from a larval to an adult form. *(metamorphosis)*
- Any closed plane figure bounded by straight lines. *(polygon)*
- Any renunciation or overthrow of one government or ruler and the substitution of another by those governed without an election and often with fighting. *(revolution)*

The Instructional Importance of Concepts

According to Bruner, Goodnow, and Austin, using concepts "is deeply imbedded in the fabric of cognitive life" (16, p. 79). As they point out in the beginning of their seminal work,

A Study of Thinking, we have the ability to discriminate and respond to so much in this life that if we did "respond to each event encountered as unique, we would soon be overwhelmed by the complexity of our environment" (16, p. 1). In order to cope with this information overload, we categorize—that is, we

> render discriminably different things equivalent . . .
> group the objects and events and people around us into
> classes, and . . . respond to them in terms of their class
> membership rather than their uniqueness. (16, p. 1)

In other words, we formulate concepts. In doing so, we render our lives more manageable in that we do not have to learn a new label for each insect we encounter, each new truck we see on the road, or each example of humor we experience. As we walk through life, our brains search for sameness in order to make perception manageable. We build a knowledge network, a schemata of concepts on which we can hang our experiences.

This utility factor is true also in teaching and learning. We cannot afford the time to present to students all of the instances of "insects" or "verbs" they may experience in life, so we teach them, through a few examples, the concepts, so they can apply them to each new experience, in or outside our classroom.

Gagne also reminds us that by using concepts students are "freed from the control of specific stimuli in [the] environment, and can thereafter learn by means of verbal instruction, presented orally or in printed form" (31, p. 137). Students can then communicate with each other and their teachers through a set of shared concepts, and they can comprehend a text that relates to concepts already within their knowledge networks. When students do not share common concepts with their teachers, authors, and peers, communication breaks down and learning becomes difficult or impossible.

One of the common mistakes teachers make is that they expect or assume students will learn concepts incidentally, as a by-product of lessons. If concepts are to be used correctly in new situations, students must receive explicit, direct instruction (50). This requires teachers first to identify the concepts of the upcoming unit, then to plan lessons that include the direct teaching of these fundamental concepts via the inductive approach.

Planning the Inductive Approach for Concept Development

In this text, concepts are being taught to you through an inductive approach. In Chapter 1, the concept of the "inductive approach" was presented inductively; in this chapter and in Chapter 4, the concepts of "concept" and "principle" are presented inductively. Recall the steps in the inductive approach, that is, the essential attributes of the inductive approach, which you learned in Chapter 1.

1. Students examine specific examples selected by the teacher.
2. Students answer the teacher's eliciting questions.
3. Students infer the generalization(s).
4. Students apply the generalization(s) to new specifics.

Go back to Chapter 1 and for the concept *inductive approach,* identify the following:

1. What specific examples did you examine? (The three Greek Myths and Legends lesson plans.)
2. What eliciting questions were you to answer? (Purpose for Reading, p. 11.)
3. What generalizations about the essential attributes of the inductive approach were derived? (Four steps given above; also see pp. 16–17.)
4. What were the application activities? (Identification/ Analysis and Guided Practice activities at the end of the chapter.)

Can you identify the steps in the inductive approach being used in this chapter to teach you the concept of *concept?* The

Readiness section gave you the eliciting questions and Lists A and B gave you the specific examples to examine in order to arrive at generalizations concerning the essential attributes of *concepts*. (It should be noted that since texts do not provide an avenue for oral dialogue between author [teacher] and reader [learner], we must ultimately give in an expository manner the generalizations for the concepts being taught. In a classroom setting, however, it would be the students, not the teacher, who would voice the generalizations. The teacher may verify the students' generalizations as either correct or incorrect.)

When planning a lesson that will use the inductive approach to teach a concept, you need to do the following:

1. Identify and analyze the essential attributes of a concept, and then state the generalization you desire students to reach.
2. Select appropriate examples of the concept for students to examine.
3. Write the eliciting questions that will guide the students in the examination of the examples and the induction of the generalization.
4. Devise the application activity that will provide evidence of students' mastery of the concept.

Essential Attributes of a Concept

Essential attributes are those common characteristics that every example in the category shares. For example, *metamorphosis* has the following essential attributes: (1) a developmental process; (2) common to insects and amphibians; (3) characterized by an abrupt, hormonally induced and regulated transformation from a larval to an adult form. Every process that is a *metamorphosis* has these essential attributes. It is crucial to understand the essential attributes of concepts you wish to teach in order to write activities or lessons that will lead students efficiently and effectively to learn the concepts. The moral "If you're not sure where you're going, you're liable to end up someplace else" is appropriate here (60, p. 1). It is the essential attributes that students should discern in an inductively taught concept activity; therefore, it is crucial that you know what they are.

As you are planning to teach a concept inductively and identifying its essential attributes, be aware that some concepts do not lend themselves to an absolute list of attributes. For example, the attributes of the concept *freedom* may be open to debate within the social studies classroom. And the attributes of a *living organism* may attract some difference of opinion in a science class. In these cases, the teacher may decide to encourage students to debate the issue, and use any defensible, student-generated list of essential attributes as acceptable. Or in the case of the concept *effective narration,* the English teacher might decide to focus attention on one or two generally accepted essential attributes, such as "show, don't tell," and "one place in time." Even when teachers believe they have identified the absolute essential attributes of a concept during planning, students often offer ideas in class that reveal the teacher's set to be inaccurate or incomplete. As one teacher said, "Students always seem to give better essential attributes than I write."

Essential attributes are of two kinds—variable and critical attributes (63) (see figure 3.2). "Variable attributes" are general attributes that place the concept into some general class. For example, the variable attribute for "polygon" is "closed, plane figure." The variable attribute is a class that can be shared by other concepts as well. For example, a "circle" is also a "closed, plane figure," but it is not a polygon. A circle is not a polygon because it does not possess the "critical attribute" for polygons, "bounded by straight lines." Critical attributes are the "differentia"—they differentiate examples from other examples that might belong to a similar class. Examples of a concept that may share a variable attribute, but not all the required critical attributes, are nonexamples of a concept. For example, a circle is a nonexample of a polygon because it is a closed plane figure (thus sharing the variable attribute); but because it is not "bounded by straight lines," it does not share the critical attribute. (It should be mentioned here that text glossaries and dictionaries often confuse students when their definitions do not provide all the critical attributes of a concept. That is why students often use erroneous words as synonyms.)

During the planning stage, it is important to recognize, too, that examples of a concept will also possess nonessential attributes (47) that might distract students from generalizing the

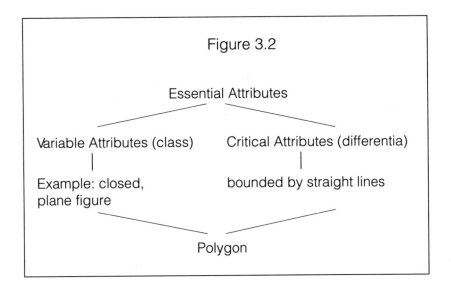

essential attributes correctly. For example, a polygon is a polygon regardless of the number of straight lines it has. Consideration of such nonessential attributes will help you eventually select examples that will lead students to efficient and accurate learning of the concept. In the case of the polygon, you should include figures that have three, four, and more sides to show that number of sides is nonessential to the generalization of the concept *polygon*.

Also, in this stage of planning as you are becoming

intimate with the concept and its nuances, you should determine if the concept under consideration has only one, or more than one, set of essential attributes when used in your discipline. For example, the concept *grand slam* in baseball has only one set of essential attributes—hitting a home run when the bases are loaded. The concept *error* in baseball, however, can be a mistake charged when a fly ball is dropped OR a mistake charged when an infielder makes a wild throw to first base. In the English class, students encounter the concept *sonnet,* which can have several different sets of essential attributes depending on the type of sonnet presented.

Concept labels can also have different essential attributes, depending on the discipline in which they are used. For example, students might have learned in their physical education class the concept label *court* for the playing field used in games like tennis, volleyball, or basketball. When they come to English class, they will learn the concept of *courting a lady.* And those who have learned the concept *cataract* in health class as it relates to care of the eyes might be confused with the introduction of *cataract* in geography class as it relates to a type of waterfall. If, during your planning, you anticipate the nonspecific nature of the concept label, you will be in a better position to prepare an activity with fewer distractions and less interference to students' memory. Sometimes, just having students recall the essential attributes of the concept they are familiar with, and acknowledging that they will now learn a different set of essential attributes for that concept label, facilitates learning.

Finally, you need to examine concepts to determine if students have the background of experience to identify and understand the essential attributes. For example, before students can learn the concept *number* in English, they must know the prerequisite concepts *verb, noun, pronoun, demonstrative adjective, singular,* and *plural.*

To summarize, during the planning stage, first clearly specify the concept to be taught, then consider its essential attributes. You must fully understand the nature of the concept in order to help students learn it. The following steps might help you delineate the essential attributes of a concept:

1. List the essential attributes of the concept.
2. Does your list of essential attributes include the variable attributes (class) and all the critical attributes (differentia)?
3. Is there an absolute list of attributes, or will the essential attributes be debatable (as they are for *freedom*)?
4. What nonessential attributes might distract the students from accurate conceptualization?
5. Does the concept have more than one set of essential attributes in this discipline?
6. Is this concept label used in any other discipline with a different set of essential attributes?
7. Have students mastered the prerequisite concepts needed to learn this new concept?
8. Now write the desired generalization about the concept that you wish students to be able to state and apply as a result of your inductive lesson.

Examples

It is in this planning stage that you select the examples of the concept that you will present to students. Example selection is crucial to the success of the inductive lesson. Bruner, Goodnow, and Austin (16) report that good examples become the focus for learners—the exemplars of a concept—a reference for them as they apply the concept in new situations.

The first requirement is that each example must contain all the essential attributes of the concept. Such examples help the learner to distinguish sameness among examples.

The second requirement is that examples contain as few nonessential attributes ("noisy" attributes) as is possible so as not to distract learners from identifying the appropriate essential attributes. Your purpose is to draw attention to the sameness among the examples without undo cognitive strain on the part of the learner (18). Examples should be sequenced for presentation from simple—few nonessential attributes—to complex—more nonessential attributes (16).

Recall the development of the concept *classical hero* in Chapter 1. Two examples of classical heroes—Theseus and Perseus—were presented to students. Both stories contained all the essential attributes of the concept, and neither hero was portrayed as having distinguishing features significantly different from the other (nonessential attributes). By selecting clear examples, the teacher focuses students' attention on essential attributes of the concept and ensures learning of the concept.

Also consider how many examples should be presented to students. Research and wisdom of practice do not reveal an easy rule for this (82). Obviously, more than one example is needed since students are discerning similarities. But as demonstrated in the classical hero example, sometimes as few as two good examples can be effective. At other times, several are required. For instance, the mathematics teacher who wishes to teach the concept *polygon* inductively needs to present several examples with varying numbers of sides to rule out the idea that a specific number of sides is an essential attribute. Avoid adding more examples for the sake of presenting a large number, however, because with each new example also comes "noise"—nonessential attributes that can distract students from inferring the essential ones.

It should be obvious by now that in this inductive approach, you deliberately select examples that will guarantee success for students in learning the concept. You are the mediator, guiding students, focusing their attention on carefully selected examples so that they can arrive at valid generalizations. This type of mediation appears to be necessary for efficient learning (32), and such success fosters favorable attitudes toward learning (49).

To further guarantee student success in inferring the generalizations from the examples, consider the use of matrices. Refer to Figure 1.1 in Chapter 1, which students complete as they read the two myths. This chart helps students focus their attention on the concept's essential attributes (68). It provides them with a visual pathway for noticing similarities between examples.

Many theorists and practitioners advocate presenting nonexamples along with examples to discourage students from forming hasty generalizations and to help them identify the essential attributes through contrast. This approach to induction is often referred to as "concept attainment" (e.g., 15, 47, 79).

The concept *polygon,* for example, has been taught successfully by presenting examples and nonexamples concurrently. The mathematics teacher displays one group of figures labeled *All These Figures Are Polygons* and another group of figures labeled *None of These Figures Are Polygons* (see Figure 3.3).

In the English class, a teacher could present two lists, one labeled *All These Sentences Contain Appositive Phrases* and another list labeled *None of These Sentences Contain Appositive Phrases.* The students would be asked to list the essential attributes of an *appositive phrase.*

All These Sentences Contain Appositive Phrases
1. Jane, our representative, met with the principal.
2. The most coveted gem, a diamond, is extremely expensive.
3. The little boy quickly fell asleep next to Bernie, the family's old sheep dog.
4. Daphne spotted the old man, George's grandfather.

None of These Sentences Contain Appositive Phrases
5. In the end, Sally bought the first car she had test-driven.
6. A sonnet is a poem of 14 lines.
7. Jane met with the principal. Jane is our representative.

Figure 3.3

List A

All These Figures Are Polygons

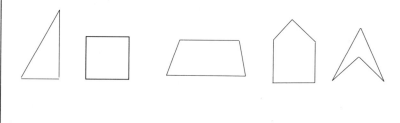

   1   2   3   4   5

List B

None of These Figures Are Polygons

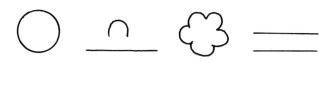

   1   2   3   4

Nonexamples can also be kept and later used as the test of mastery of the concept. For example, in Chapter 1, Mrs. Carter could have had students read the disparate nonexample, "The Most Dangerous Game," and explain why its central character is not a *classical hero* by contrasting each of the essential attributes of the concept. Or a social studies teacher, after inductively teaching the concept *metropolis*, might show students a series of slides (e.g., of downtown Chicago, an aerial view of the Sahara desert, a midwestern ranch, an aerial view of New York City and its surrounding suburbs) and ask students to decide which show metropolises, using their established list of essential attributes for their defense. Their responses would indicate to the teacher the degree of student mastery of the concept.

Another choice you must make is whether to introduce two concepts simultaneously because of their close relationship in your discipline. For example, a science teacher might want to teach the related concepts *solid* and *liquid* concurrently (33). The teacher could first show a container of water and tell students, "This is a liquid," then show a rock and say, "This is a solid." These two examples would be followed by similar simultaneous presentations using substances such as powdered sugar and milk, and wood and motor oil. A social studies teacher might choose this simultaneous approach for the related concepts *propaganda* and *fact*; the English teacher for *simile* and *metaphor;* the mathematics teacher for *set* and *empty set.* Be cautioned, however, not to try to do too much too fast. Presenting related concepts simultaneously or separately will depend on the number and complexity of the essential attributes, the ability level of your students, and the time available for teaching the lesson.

It should be obvious by now that you may use many types of media to present examples (and nonexamples) to students in order to help them learn concepts. Middle and high school students are quite capable of learning concepts through examples presented in appropriate-level reading materials or in lecture format by the teacher. Many concepts lend themselves to examples that are iconic in nature—that is, models, slides, still pictures, demonstrations. Audio recordings, too, might be used. Such media also add variety to instruction and allow students with different learning styles and modalities to improve their chances of mastering the concept. Regardless of the medium chosen, students should have direct experience with examples if they are to achieve an understanding of the concept effectively and efficiently.

The following checklist can help you verify the examples you use:

1. Decide whether the examples should be presented through reading; lecture; demonstration; examination of models, pictures, or slides; listening to a recording, or some other more appropriate medium.
2. Check each example you select to ensure that it contains all the essential attributes of the concept.
3. Pretend you do not know the concept to be attained. How else could your examples be categorized? What example could you add to rule out this generalization?
4. Identify the nonessential attributes in each of your examples. Will it help your students if you sequence the examples from simple (few nonessential attributes) to complex (several nonessential attributes)?
5. Consider the number of examples you have selected. Is the number sufficient to help students discern all the essential attributes, but not so many that unnecessary "noise" distracts students?
6. Does the nature of the concept lend itself to using a matrix that would help students focus on the concept's essential attributes.
7. Select nonexamples of the concept. Decide whether these nonexamples will be presented simultaneously with the examples, or whether they would be more appropriately used later as a check for students' mastery

of the concept.

8. Is there another concept that should be taught simultaneously due to interrelatedness of the two concepts? Is a simultaneous presentation appropriate, considering the complexity of the essential attributes of the concepts, the ability of students, and the time available to teach the lesson?

Eliciting Questions and Generalizations

At this stage in your planning, you should understand fully the nuances of the concept you wish to teach, and know what the final outcome—the generalization of the essential attributes—should be for your students' task. But now you must decide how you will get them to this outcome, and much of "getting them there" depends on your skills in questioning. Since at this point in the lesson you will be primarily a questioner, planning the key eliciting questions you will ask is critical to students' success. Your eliciting questions will require your students to infer relationships and to make generalizations. Hilda Taba, one of the pioneers in the study and application of the inductive approach, and her associates cautioned that "these [reasoning] skills are not an automatic by-product of maturation and experience . . . " (79, p. 109). Therefore, we must be patient if at first our students seem to struggle. One classroom teacher summarized it this way,

> When I began using the inductive approach with my students, it was very difficult for them. It was as if they had never ever thought this way before. But after a while it seemed to become second nature to them. They even began to anticipate my questions.

Following are the series of directions and questions used by the teachers who taught the concepts *polygon* and *appositive phrase*. (Refer to pages 44–46 for the examples and nonexamples.) Also reexamine Mrs. Carter's lesson on *classical heroes* from Chapter 1. What questions are the same for each lesson? How do

48

the questions differ for each lesson?

Concept: Polygon

Directions and eliciting questions prepared by the teacher to guide students:

1. "Examine carefully each of the figures in Lists A and B." (See Figure 3.3.)
2. "How are the figures in List B different from those in List A?" (List B has open figures and figures with curved lines.)
   [Be prepared to cue students with these questions, if necessary, in order to help them notice the differences—"How are Figures 1, 2, and 3 from List B different from all the figures in List A?" "How are 2 and 4 in List B different from all the figures in List A?"]
3. "How are all the figures in List A alike?" (All have straight lines; all are closed.)
4. Display a cube and a rectangular box. Tell students, "These models have straight lines and are closed figures, yet neither is a polygon. How are these models different from the figures in List A?" (They are plane figures—not three-dimensional.)
5. Have each student write his/her own generalization into a concluding statement that includes the three essential attributes of a *polygon*. Listen to several responses. Write the consensus generalization on the chalkboard.

Concept: Appositive Phrase

1. Review—"Recall what a *phrase* is. Is it a complete sentence or part of a sentence? Who will give an example of a sentence that contains a phrase?" Write

49

this phrase on the board. Ask for one or two additional examples.

2. "Read the seven examples on the paper in front of you. The first four are examples of sentences with *appositive phrases;* sentences 5–7 do not contain *appositives.*"

3. "How are sentences 1–4 similar? How are they different from 5–7? The answer has to do with the construction of each sentence, not with its meaning." [Be prepared to cue students to recognize the new kind of phrase by reminding them that an appositive phrase is a phrase; therefore, they should carefully examine the phrases contained in each sentence.]

4. "Underline the appositive phrases in sentences 1–4."

5. "Now may I have volunteers tell us what phrases they underlined?"
[The teacher underlines appositive phrase on an overhead transparency as students respond.]

6. "With what part of speech does each appositive phrase end?" (Noun.) "Each appositive begins with what type of word?" (A noun marker—article or possessive.)

7. "What is each appositive phrase doing to the meaning of each sentence? That is, what is it adding?" (An explanation or identification of another noun in the sentence.)

8. "Where is an appositive phrase placed within a sentence?" (Beside the noun it is describing or explaining.)

9. Have each student write his/her own generalization into a concluding statement that includes the four essential attributes of an appositive phrase. Listen to several responses. Write the final group consensus on the transparency.

In the two preceding lesson plan segments, both teachers

gave similar types of directions and questions. First, they instructed students to examine the data (facts) carefully—look at the math figures and read the English sentences. Mrs. Carter, in teaching her students the concept *classical hero* also had her students examine data (facts) carefully. She had them use a chart because of the amount of data contained in the two myths. Second, each teacher asked students to identify differences (to contrast) and similarities (to compare) among the data.

Notice that the teachers prepared additional questions to ask if the students did not readily infer the similarities and differences. (For example, see the *polygon* lesson, question 2.) Experience has shown that students of lower ability and those inexperienced in the inductive approach require more pointed eliciting questions to guide them toward the generalization than do students of higher ability or those experienced in inductive learning.

Although during this stage of the lesson preparation you will carefully think through your eliciting questions, you should be prepared to adapt or add questions during the actual teaching if students need additional direction or clarification. The questions you prepare are key questions; they are crucial to the success of the inductive approach. They should not, however, be interpreted as a script, which cannot be rewritten if the questions are not producing the desired outcome. If you thoroughly understand the concept you are teaching, you should be able to adapt your questions as necessary, while still focusing on similarities and differences. Sometimes you may find that your examples and nonexamples are not valid, and that you must add or delete some in the midst of a lesson, especially if this is the first time you have attempted to teach a particular concept via the inductive approach. Patience, flexibility, and clarity are the benchmarks of the inductive teacher!

Notice also that it is the students (not the teachers) who in all three lessons—*classical heroes, polygons,* and *appositive phrases*—state the generalization by summarizing the essential attributes of the concept into a single concluding statement. It is advisable to have students write out their own statements first, as opposed to just orally sharing them, so that they can see their generalizations in writing and revise them if necessary. The teacher then displays the generalization visually—on the chalkboard or the overhead projector—so that all students can contribute to the final version and can make a copy for themselves for later review.

Because students have been allowed to state the generalization in their own words, it should be understandable to them since it originates from their linguistic networks. If you want to expand students' content vocabulary at this time, you may want to introduce a new term for the one that the students provided. For example, if in learning *polygon,* students had used "two-dimensional" in their description of one of the essential attributes, at this point in the inductive approach, the teacher may tell them that in mathematics, this is also referred to as a "plane" figure.

Once consensus has been reached on the wording of the generalization, you should tell students the *label* for the concept they have just learned—assuming, of course, that the label was not identified earlier in the lesson. Remember that Mrs. Carter saved the label *classical hero* until after writing the generalization, whereas the other two teachers used the labels *polygon* and *appositive phrase* from the beginning of the lessons. Although many writers advocate saving the concept label until after the generalization, many practitioners will argue that identifying the label early in the lesson is not detrimental to the value of the inductive approach.

Finally, in this planning phase, you might want to consider having students work in pairs, triads, or small groups in order to provide a tutorial atmosphere and to capitalize on the positive effects of talking and collaborative learning, while students attempt to identify similarities and differences and to arrive at a generalization. Recall that Mrs. Carter had her students work in pairs to compare the facts recorded on their charts and to note similarities between Perseus and Theseus. It is possible that for some groups of students, learning the concepts *polygon* and *appositive phrase* could be facilitated with discussion groups followed by an entire-class discussion to reach consensus on the generalization.

The following questions should help you plan appropriate eliciting questions and directions for helping students use their inductive reasoning to generalize the concept:

1. Have I directed students to examine the facts carefully?
2. Have I asked students to note differences?
3. Have I asked students to note similarities that all the examples share?
4. Have I prepared additional eliciting questions that focus students' attention on essential attributes?
5. Would it facilitate conceptualization if students worked on these questions in pairs, triads, or small groups before an entire-class discussion for consensus ensues?
6. Have I planned to let my *students* phrase the generalization? Will I encourage them to write out their generalizations before they share them orally with the entire class?
7. Where will I record the suggested generalizations so as a class we can examine and revise them if necessary in order to reach consensus?
8. Are there any content-specific words in the generalization that I have written during this planning that I will want to introduce to students if they do not include the term in their summary statement?

Application Activity

The real test of whether students have indeed learned a concept is if they can apply their new knowledge. Tests of conceptual mastery can take several forms. One used most often at the conclusion of the initial teaching of the concept is to give students new examples (and if appropriate, nonexamples) and have them discriminate if each is an example of the concept. They must, of course, cite the presence or absence of the concept's essential attributes in defending their decisions. The mathematics teacher who taught the concept *polygon* might choose to test for mastery by distributing a sheet containing three new figures and asking students to write a defense for their decision as to whether or not each figure is a *polygon*. The science teacher might prepare a similar handout with a list of substances that students would classify as *solids* or *liquids*, after an inductive lesson on these concepts. Mrs. Carter asked her students to decide whether Jason was a *classical hero*.

Sometimes, concepts lend themselves to application tests that require students to change nonexamples to examples. The English teacher might give students several nonexamples of appositive phrases such as the following:

Jane met with the principal. Jane is our representative.

and instruct them to combine the sentences in order to include an appositive phrase, thus converting each nonexample into an example. As these new examples are shared, students should be required to defend their rewrites on the basis of the essential attributes of *appositive phrases*.

Concept mastery can sometimes be tested by asking students to find their own examples of the concept and to defend their choices, again using the essential attributes. For example, the mathematics students might have been asked to look through magazines, find two examples of *polygons* used in advertising, and write a defense of their choices.

Students might also demonstrate learning of the concept by creating their own examples of the concept. The mathematics students could draw new polygons; the English students could include appositive phrases in their current compositions.

At an advanced level of mastery, we would expect that our

students could use their newly acquired concepts later when additional, related concepts are introduced in our disciplines. For example, science students who have previously learned the concept *predator* may be asked to decide if the squid is a predator as a result of a squid dissection activity and reading.

Finally, we would expect that students who had mastered concepts would be able to use the concept labels as part of their oral and written expression. For example, in a discussion of current events in a social studies class, we would expect students who had learned the concept *revolution* to use it correctly in their description of the happenings in Nicaragua and Romania in 1990.

All these activities will reveal to you whether your students have indeed learned the concept. Notice that none of them simply asks the student to state the generalization. Such recitation is no guarantee of conceptualization. Valid tests of mastery include an application component. Therefore, as you plan the application activity that will test student mastery of the concept you presented inductively in your lesson, consider the following options:

1. Give students new examples and ask them to defend if each is an example of the concept.
2. Give students nonexamples that they must change to examples. Students must defend their changes.
3. Have students locate their own examples of the concept and defend their choices.
4. Have students create their own examples of the concept and defend their creations.

SUMMARY

As a secondary discipline teacher, you have a choice as to how the key concepts of your units will be presented. You can present concepts in an expository manner—that is, tell students what the concepts mean. Another choice is to lead students through the steps of the inductive approach, and allow them to discover the meaning of the concepts. Wisdom of experience is definitely on the side of the inductive approach for fundamental concepts of the discipline. Montague summarizes it this way:

> If properly conducted, an inductive strategy will result in more student involvement, more intrinsic interest in the lesson, better transfer of learning, and higher achievement of more complex cognitive understandings. (63, p. 149)

KNOWLEDGE CHECK

1. Refer to page 34 and answer the purpose-for-reading questions.
2. Identify the variable attributes and the critical attributes in the concept generalizations on page 35.
3. Which of the concepts on page 33 have more than one set of essential attributes?
4. What prerequisite concepts are necessary for learning the concept *absolute location?* For learning *metamorphosis?*

GUIDED PRACTICE

If possible, work with a partner who is in your same discipline. Together, select a fundamental concept from your field that you might need to teach your secondary students. Use the questions on page 42 to write the desired generalization.

Chapter 4

HOW TO USE
THE INDUCTIVE APPROACH
FOR PRINCIPLE FORMATION

READINESS

Go back to the beginning of Chapter 3 and reexamine Lists A and B. As you remember, List A is composed of labels for *concepts*; all the statements in List B are *principles*. How do *principles* differ from *concepts*? What is the relationship between a *principle* and a *concept*? (Clue—Notice the concepts *verb, number,* and *subject.* Now look carefully at the first principle in List B.) Use your knowledge of *concepts* to write the essential attributes of a *principle*.

PURPOSE FOR READING

1. What is a "principle"? Verify your prediction from the Readiness section.
2. Why are "principles" important to the disciplines?
3. What are the steps in an inductive approach to principle formation?

A *principle* is a generalization that describes relationships between and among concepts in a discipline (62). As with concepts, such generalizations are inferred from the examination of examples.

The principle *a verb should be the same number as its subject* is a statement of a relationship among the concepts *verb, number,* and *subject* in the discipline of English/Language Arts. The principle *Native American Indians have suffered from concentration policies and broken treaties* is a generalization in the discipline of social studies that states a relationship among the concepts *Native American Indians, suffered, concentration policies,* and *broken treaties.* Both principles were inferred from the examination of examples of English sentences and of Indian treaties.

Since principles are commonly the essence of knowledge in the disciplines (31) and the building blocks for future problem solving, it is crucial that students understand them and not just demonstrate the ability to "parrot" them. When teaching a principle, you have two choices as to how to present it—through the expository mode or through the inductive (discovery) mode.

Assuming that students have previously learned each of the concepts that will form the principle, you could just tell them the principle—that is, use expository instruction. This type of receptive learning is certainly the most time-efficient way to present such knowledge to students, and it is the way that many of us learn each day. For example, the teacher reads a professional journal and learns a technique to use with learning-disabled students, or the cable television servicer reads a manual and learns how to hook up wires to a television with an advanced stereo system.

However, the danger inherent in the expository approach in the classroom is that students will only form what Gagne calls "verbal chains" and not "conceptual chains" (31, p. 53). That is, students will be able to say the principle, but will not understand it and therefore not be able to apply it. For example, students who are told the principle of subject and verb agreeing in number, may be able to state the rule, but continue to misuse the rule in their own writing. Such "empty verbalism is not enough" (61, p. 42).

There is ample evidence that if students are guided to discover the principle themselves, they will better retain and more readily transfer their new knowledge (32). Students who only learn verbal chains forget them in a very short period of time, whereas students who learn principles themselves retain the knowledge (31).

58

"There is not always a positive relationship between success and textbook (expository) learning. I have had so many students who were poor textbook learners but did very well with the inductive approach for learning principles."

Therefore, in planning a unit, identify those principles that are fundamental to the unit and prerequisite to other learning, and plan lessons that develop them through the inductive approach. For example, the English teacher would be well advised to teach the fundamental principle of subject-verb agreement inductively since students will need to apply this rule for all writing they do. And the social studies teacher should teach inductively the fundamental principle *geographical features influence crop production in a region* since this principle has application to every region students will study in the future.

Planning the Inductive Approach for Principle Formation

Refer to p. 17 in Chapter 1. The lesson described there is a teacher's attempt to use the inductive approach to have students in her mathematics class learn the principle *the sum of the interior angles of a triangle is equal to 180 degrees.* First, the teacher reviewed the concepts *triangle* and *interior angle* and the processes involved in the measurement of angles. Next, students examined multiple examples of triangles. Then, guided by the teacher's eliciting questions, students measured each of the interior angles, recorded their findings on a chart, added their findings, and generalized the principle of the sum of the interior angles of any triangle. Students will apply this principle later when they study the measurement of supplementary angles.

Notice the similarity in the inductive approach for principle formation and concept development. In both, you must:

1. Determine if students have mastered prerequisites.
2. Provide appropriate examples for students to examine.
3. Ask eliciting questions that lead students to state the generalization.

4. Plan an activity that will require students to apply their learning and thus demonstrate evidence of concept development or principle formation.

Therefore, in preparing an inductively taught lesson for a principle, you will use some of the guidelines previously given for a concept, as well as some considerations unique to the teaching of principles.

Principle Prerequisites

Because a principle is a generalization that describes relationships between and among concepts, it is essential that students have already mastered the concepts inherent in the principle. Assumptive teaching—assuming that students have the necessary prerequisites—could result in students being unsuccessful in formulating the principle. For example, the mathematics students could not have been successful in generalizing that *the sum of the interior angles of a triangle is 180 degrees,* if they had not already learned the concepts *sum, interior angles, triangle,* and *degrees.*

In planning the lesson, you must first delineate these prerequisites, determine whether students do indeed know them, then decide which of the prerequisite concepts need to be taught or reviewed. If you are sure that a concept has been mastered by students and they will have no difficulty recalling it, you need not review it. This often happens when the concept is one students mastered long ago and use regularly. For example, this is probably true of the concept *sum* for the eighth grade student. The value of review will also depend on the ability level of your students. Those of lower ability sometimes require more frequent review to mobilize previously learned concepts and principles.

Some principles require students to recall and apply other prerequisite principles. For instance, when the mathematics teacher wants to teach inductively the principle *the sum of the measures of two supplementary angles is 180 degrees,* students will have to recall the previous principle *(the sum of the interior angles of a triangle is 180 degrees)* when examining examples such as those shown in Figure 4.1 and determining the angle measurements for *a* and *b*.

These guidelines will help you avoid assumptive teaching of principles:

1. Write the generalization you wish students to learn.
2. List the concepts in the generalization.
3. Have students mastered each of these concepts? (If not, how will you teach them?)
4. Do you need to review any of these concepts before introducing the examples to be examined for discovering the principle? If so, how will you review each concept with students?
5. Are prerequisite principles required for learning this new principle? If so, how will you cue students to recall these principles?

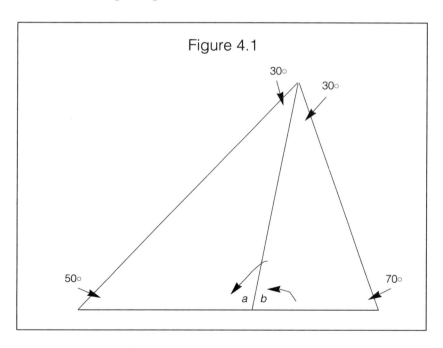

Figure 4.1

Examples

The selection of examples is a crucial step in planning an inductive lesson. The exact number will vary from principle to principle, and possibly even from class to class. The number of examples, however, should be sufficient so that students can discern a pattern and make a generalization that is appropriate for all examples—those seen and even those not seen. Notice that in the mathematics example where the generalization dealt with the sum of the interior angles of the triangle, each student worked with three triangles; therefore, even if only 20 students were in the class, they were exposed to the sums of 60 triangles.

If a social studies teacher wished to teach the principle *Native American Indians have suffered from concentration policies and broken treaties,* students might be exposed to the Indian Removal Act, the Dawes Act, and the experiences of Jim Thorpe and Chief Joseph, etc., in order to make this valid generalization (58). All the examples should help focus students' attention toward information that will support their generalization.

Taba and her colleagues (79) make an important point when they remind us that sometimes it is better to have students do an in-depth study of two contrasting examples, rather than a cursory examination of many examples. For instance, to develop the principle *life in the colonies was influenced by the settlers' religious beliefs and skills, and the geographical characteristics of their landing place,* the teacher might have students examine only two contrasting colonies (e.g., Massachusetts and South Carolina), rather than make a superficial study of all 13 colonies. The contrast pattern will present less "noise" than if all the colonies were overviewed.

Matrices can sometimes be used to assist students in collecting information and then "reading" it for similarities that will facilitate their statement of the principle. Obviously, the mathematics chart on which students recorded the degrees of each angle of their triangles, then added the sums of the angles for each triangle, gave them visual clues for recognizing that all three triangles had interior angles that added to 180 degrees.

In a science class, students can make weather observations for several weeks, recording daily data on clouds, temperature, air pressure, wind, etc., on a chart. They can then examine these charts in class to make generalizations about how wind direction and temperature changes relate to high- and low-pressure systems (17).

Similarly, the science teacher who wishes students to formulate the principle *an increasing population cannot survive in a given habitat* could have them chart the answers to the following questions:

1. There are 50 birds in a given habitat. In the first year the flock inhabits the area, there are 20,000 seeds for the flock to share each day. How many seeds will each bird have each day for this year? Record your response on a chart (see Figure 4.2).
2. By the next year, the birds have reproduced and their number now is 150. The habitat remains relatively unchanged; therefore, there are still approximately 20,000 seeds for the flock. How many seeds will each bird have each day for this year? Record your response on the chart.
3. The next year finds 375 birds in the flock, with a relatively unchanged habitat. How many seeds will each bird have each day for this year? Record your response on the chart.

Not all principles lend themselves to examples that can or need to be put into a matrix, however. For example, the English teacher who wishes to teach the principle *a verb should be the same number as its subject* would not need a chart. A list of sentences that correctly demonstrate the principle, and possibly a list of sentences that violate the principle (nonexamples), should key students into the relationship for the generalization.

Correct

1. The baby cries.
2. The dogs cry.
3. The bag of stones was heavy.

Incorrect

1. The baby cry.
2. The dogs cries.
3. The bag of stones were heavy.

What is the grammatical principle demonstrated above?

It should be obvious by now that many types of media can be used as the source of information for students to examine. In a social studies lesson about life on southern plantations, students would most likely gather their facts from text reading or a filmstrip. In a science lesson about wind and pressure changes, students would make direct observations of weather conditions. In the English lesson about subject-verb agreement, students would examine examples and nonexamples that the teacher prepared. A social studies lesson that attempts to formulate a principle concerning values in the 1880s and 1920s might have students examine pictures from each of the time periods (27).

Role-playing can also be used to help students infer a principle. For example, in science class, students can role play grasshopper nymphs and adults and butterfly larvae and adults that demonstrate the differences in eating habits within the groups. By observing what happens when each group goes

Figure 4.2		
Year	Number of Birds	Seeds Per Bird
1	50	
2	150	
3	375	

toward its favorite food, students are readily able to infer that *insects exhibiting complete metamorphosis do not compete for food* (30).

Some inductive lessons for principle formation require students to use multiple sources for their information. For example, in establishing the principle about Native American Indians suffering from concentration policies and broken treaties, the teacher may want to arrange a series of readings, or give a lecture, then supplement this with a movie or filmstrip about the plight of the Indians. And the lesson on life in the colonies being affected by the beliefs of the colonists and the geographical conditions of the area could use readings, filmstrips, and maps to provide the facts upon which students would infer the generalization.

Sometimes the examples come directly from students. This could happen in an English class where reader-response is so crucial. Students need to use their background experiences and beliefs when encountering literary text. Therefore, the teacher may ask students to respond to a piece by writing in their journals what they think a poem is about, why they think a particular novel is considered a "classic," what they think the significance of a particular line in a short story is, or what statement about life a piece is conveying. Student responses then become the examples of interpretation, and through discussion, debate, justification, reexamination, and teacher guidance, similarities and differences are determined and a class interpretation (generalization) may be induced.

The following checklist can help you verify the examples you choose:

1. Decide whether the examples should be presented through reading; lecture; demonstration; role-playing; examination of models, pictures, or slides; listening to a recording; student-generated examples; or some other appropriate medium.

2. Check each example to be sure the generalization can be inferred from it.
3. Consider the number of examples you will use. Provide enough to make the pattern obvious, while not confusing students with additional "noise."
4. Consider whether the principle lends itself to the use of a matrix for collecting the facts.

Eliciting Questions and Generalizations

You must now plan the help students will need to process the examples in order to maximize efficient discovery of the generalization—the statement of the principle. Again, as with concept development, you will primarily be a director and questioner.

In the mathematics lesson on the sum of the interior angles of a triangle, the teacher directed students to cut out three triangles, label the interior angles, measure each angle, then record their measurements on their chart. When this was completed, she instructed them to add the angles of each triangle and record the sum on their charts. She then took on the role of questioner by asking each student to report his/her sum for each angle. The repetition of the answer "180 degrees" from each student made the pattern obvious; therefore, when she asked for the principle—"What then can we conclude about the angles of any size triangle?"—the students should have had no difficulty stating the generalization.

The science teacher who wanted his students to learn the principle *an increasing population cannot survive in a given habitat* (see p. 63) asked questions that required students to perform some basic mathematics in order to determine and record on a chart the number of seeds per bird as the population increased. The teacher led the students through three years of bird population increase so they would see from their charts that the number of seeds per bird was decreasing with each annual increase of birds in a stable habitat. To focus students' attention on this the teacher asked, "Look at the second column of your chart. What is happening to the number of birds from year 1 to year 2 to year 3? Now look at the third column of your chart. What is happening to the number of seeds per bird from year 1 to year 2 to year 3?" (It should be noted that some students may need more years to discern the pattern.) The teacher then asked, "Therefore, what can we say about the relationship between the number of birds and the number of seeds in a given, unchanging habitat?" Finally, the teacher would ask, "What would eventually happen to the birds in this habitat?"

In a social studies lesson in which students examine pictures or slides depicting the 1800s and 1920s to formulate a principle concerning the values of each time period, the teacher would probably begin by having students examine the pictures depicting the 1800s and asking, "What is happening in this picture? What are the people doing? What are they wearing? (Repeat for each picture.) What do these pictures tell you about the people of this era and what they valued?" This same procedure would be followed for the set of pictures depicting the 1920s. Follow-up questions (such as, "How are the values of the people of these two eras the same? different?") would call students' attention to similarities and differences, leading to the generalization.

Your role is always the same during this phase of the inductive approach to principle formation. First, you must help your students carefully examine and discriminate information in the examples; then you must ask eliciting questions that focus their attention on the patterns that lead to the formulation of the generalization. In this way, you facilitate the use of students' inductive reasoning, which leads to success in formulating and learning the principle.

As with concept development, you need to prepare your questions, but you should also be prepared during the actual teaching of the lesson to adapt or add to your questions if students need more or less assistance to accomplish the goal of stating the principle. Also, since in the inductive approach it is the students, not the teacher, who put the principle into words, be prepared to accept a principle statement that may convey the same meaning, but may not be identical in wording to that which you originally planned. For example, *when you add the three interior angles of a triangle, you always get 180 degrees* for all intents and purposes is the same as *the sum of the interior angles of a triangle equals 180 degrees;* because it is in the students' language, it may be more understandable for transfer. You will need to consider carefully whether it is important to impose your wording on their principle.

Some teachers report that when they first begin using the inductive approach for principle formation with lower-ability students or those for whom inductive reasoning has not been a regular part of their schooling, they give students fill-in-the-blank generalizations to complete, as opposed to requiring them to generate the entire principle on their own. For example, the mathematics teacher may provide the following:

> *When you add the three _____ _____ of a triangle, you always get _____.*

These teachers report that such completion activities seem to help students understand what a generalization is, and eventually students are able to generate principles on their own.

Finally, in this phase of the planning, consider if collaborative learning would facilitate student learning of the principle. For example, the directions and questions for the mathematics lesson on the sum of the interior angles of the triangle might have been typed on a ditto, and students could have worked in pairs, or groups of three or four, to complete the steps and arrive at the generalization before an entire-class discussion for consensus ensued. Through collaborative learning, students for whom the topic and use of inductive reasoning may be difficult could be assisted by their more proficient peers. The teacher would also have an opportunity to circulate among groups and provide some individualized attention, which is not always possible when he/she is guiding an entire-class discussion.

The following questions will help you plan appropriate directions and eliciting questions so that students may use inductive reasoning effectively to generalize the principle:

1. Have I planned questions that direct students to examine the facts carefully?
2. Have I asked students to notice similarities (and differences if appropriate)?
3. Would it facilitate the principle formulation if students worked in pairs, triads, or small groups before an entire-class discussion for consensus ensues?
4. Have I planned to let my students phrase the principle? Do they need the assistance of a fill-in-the-blank generalization? Will I encourage them to write out their generalizations before they share them with the entire class?
5. Where will I record the suggested principles so as a class we can examine and revise in order to reach consensus?
6. Which aspects of the principle statement I have prepared must be in the students' principle statement for it to be valid?

Application Activity

The final step in the inductive approach is having students apply the principle they have learned to new data. If they can successfully make this transfer, they will demonstrate principle formation. The nature of the application activity depends on what you expect your students ultimately to be able to do with their newly formed principle. For example, the mathematics teacher has as the final goal that students will be able to apply the principle of the sum of interior angles to find the degrees of an angle when given the degrees for the other two interior angles, and to apply this principle again when they must find the degrees of an interior angle that is also a supplementary angle. Therefore, the application activities will be two: practice problems immediately after the generalization of the principle for which students must independently calculate the degrees for the third angle when the degrees for the first two angles are provided; and calculations of the same type in a later lesson when students are discerning the sum of supplementary angles. One is immediate, the other in a future lesson. Both, however, require that students now work independently, so the teacher can decide if they have mastered the principle.

Sometimes you will want to first *provide* an activity that requires students to apply the principle, then instruct them to *create* their own examples that demonstrate the principle. For example, the English teacher who has taught the principle of subject and verb agreeing in number may first want students to use the principle to select verbs when given sentences like the following:

1. One of the cakes (taste/tastes) like strawberries.
2. Yesterday you (was/were) asking for the car keys.

Once the teacher is satisfied with the results of this activity that this principle has been learned, she could hold students accountable for applying the rule independently during the writing of their own compositions (the ultimate goal for this principle formation).

Often principle formation can be tested by having students use the principle as the basis for a prediction activity. For example, a teacher who wishes students to formulate the principle *economically depressed countries have a greater likelihood of experiencing a political revolution* might have students gather data on the average personal income, gross national product (GNP), life expectancy, population growth, imports versus exports, etc., of several countries that have recently experienced a political revolution (e.g., China, Afghanistan, East Germany, Lithuania, Nicaragua) and several countries that have not

70

recently experienced a political revolution (e.g., the United States, England, Sweden, Switzerland). The application activity for this principle might have students select another country in the world today that they would predict might be a candidate for a revolution by explaining its economic situation (90). It should be noted here that, depending on the ability of the students, or the perceived success of the lesson, this social studies teacher might first provide another country and its data for students to defend as either a likely or unlikely candidate for a revolution, before asking them to independently apply the principle by identifying a country of their choosing with its supporting data.

It is important to remember that just because students can state the principle is no guarantee that they have learned its meaning. On the other hand, if students can demonstrate that they can independently apply the principle, they will be demonstrating that they have indeed learned the principle.

Ask yourself the following questions as you prepare the application activity to test for principle formation:

1. What is my purpose in teaching this principle? What do I want my students ultimately to be able to do with this knowledge? How can I fashion that goal into an application activity?
2. Should I first provide examples for my students to use to apply the principle? Should students apply the principle to examples of their own creation?
3. Does the application activity require students to do more than just state the principle?

SUMMARY

Research, theory, and wisdom of practice support the principle that *the inductive approach should be used to teach fundamental concepts and principles in the secondary academic disciplines.* Students learn the content of the disciplines while getting practice using their inductive reasoning skills.

71

Notice, too, that the inductive teaching approach, as it has been operationally defined in this text, can also give students practice in deductive reasoning—beginning with a generalization and then supporting that generalization with specifics. Can you discern when that can happen within the inductive teaching approach? Examine the application activity examples presented in the previous chapters that involve students in applying a generalization by providing the specifics for new examples of the generalization.

KNOWLEDGE CHECK

1. Go back to the beginning of this chapter and answer the three purpose-for-reading questions.
2. Compare and contrast a *concept* and a *principle.*

GUIDED PRACTICE

If possible, work with a partner who is in your discipline and complete the following activities:

1. Using the principles listed at the beginning of Chapter 3, pp. 33–34, list the concepts that make up each principle.
2. Using only the principles on pp. 33 and 34 that are from your discipline, determine if prerequisite principles are required for learning each new principle.
3. Select a fundamental principle from your discipline that you might teach your secondary students. Answer the questions on page 61.

Chapter 5

INDUCTIVE REASONING IN ENGLISH

> Last week I used an inductive approach to teach
> compound sentences with conjunctive adverbs. I
> expected my students to be able to tell me the
> characteristics of the concept and to write original
> sentences in their own writing. If I were interested in their
> knowledge remaining at the identification level and not at
> the application level, I may have chosen a deductive
> approach ... But if I want the students to know from
> "roots out," as opposed to the "flowers in," I use
> induction. (2)

READINESS

The discipline of English provides teachers with opportunities to encourage students to use inductive reasoning in literature, composition, and language lessons. There are concepts and principles fundamental to each of these three components of the discipline. To help you apply what you have learned thus far in this book specifically to the teaching of English, complete the chart with concepts and principles fundamental to the teaching of literature, composition, and language (see Figure 5.1). If possible, share your completed chart with a colleague in the field of English.

PURPOSE FOR READING

Following are descriptions of two inductively presented English lessons. The first is a prewriting lesson on personality profiles; the second is a language minilesson on punctuating dialogue within a narrative piece. As you read, note the following for each lesson:

1. What concept or principle is being learned?
2. What examples are examined by students?
3. What eliciting questions does the teacher ask?
4. What generalization is made?
5. What application activity is used to test students' mastery of the concept or principle?

Lesson 1. Prewriting Lesson for Personality Profile Composition (Grade 11)

The teacher begins the class by telling students that their focus question for the day is "What are the specifications for writing a 'Personality Profile'?" She then distributes four pieces of writing, identifying three of them as "Personality Profiles" and the fourth as a "Factual Biography." All four are compositions written by eleventh graders in previous classes.

The teacher instructs her students to read the four writings in order to determine: "What do the personality profiles have in common?" "How are the personality profiles different from a factual biography?" and therefore, "What are the specifications for writing a personality profile?" Students are instructed to develop their own responses first, then to work with their

Figure 5.1

	Concept	Principle
Teaching Literature		
Teaching Composition		
Teaching Language		

assigned partners to share responses and attempt to reach consensus. As students read, think, and discuss, the teacher circulates throughout the room, asking directive questions as needed to facilitate their success. (For example, to one group whose members believe their list of specifications is complete, she asks, "Do you notice any differences between the personality profiles and factual biography in terms of their description of the individual's appearance?")

When the groups have completed their work, the teacher leads an entire-class discussion that results in agreement on the following list of specifications for the content of a personality profile.

A "Personality Profile" includes:

1. a description of specific actions/behaviors that highlight interesting or idiosyncratic aspects of the person's personality;
2. a description of aspects of the person's appearance that seem to reveal his/her personality;
3. quotes by others about the individual that give insight into the person's personality;
4. quotes from the individual that reveal his/her personality.

The positive effect of these specifications is discussed as each is presented and agreed upon. The teacher then gives students another personality profile to read. She describes this one as having a "flaw"—that is, it is missing one of the specifications. After reading the profile, students recognize that this personality profile does not include quotes from the individual about whom it is written. The effect of this omission is discussed to highlight the importance of including this specification in the personality profiles.

As the class draws to a close, the teacher informs the students that these are the specifications that should be in the personality profiles that they are going to write. She has each student choose a classmate about whom he/she will write a personality profile. Tomorrow, students will prepare their interview questions that will provide them with initial information for writing their profiles.

In this lesson, students learn the concept *personality profile* (61). Writings that are personality profiles can be grouped together because they share certain common characteristics—essential attributes. It is these attributes that the teacher has students generate as "specifications" for their own writing. In order to facilitate students' successful generalization of these specifications for writing a personality profile, the teacher asked the following eliciting questions: "What do the personality profiles have in common?" and "How are the personality profiles different from the factual biography?" The teacher also asked additional eliciting questions as deemed necessary as she circulated among groups to note their progress in writing the generalization (the specifications of a personality profile).

Notice that the teacher presented the examples and the nonexample simultaneously. The students read four pieces—three personality profile models to help them discern commonalities and one factual biography to highlight the essential attributes through contrast. (For example, the factual biography had no quotes from interviews with the person or others who knew him/her, as did all the personality profiles. The factual biography included a litany of events in the person's life; the personality profiles contained no such encompassing historical overview.) The teacher selected the personality profile examples carefully, making sure that each included all the specifications she wished the students to discover.

This lesson contained two application activities. The first had students identify the missing specification from a new personality profile, but the real test to determine if students can transfer their knowledge will be to write their own personality profiles of classmates. The specifications will be their guides and may be used by the teacher in evaluating students' writings.

The interaction in this lesson should also be noticed. Students read silently and first attempted the generalization alone; then they worked with partners and finally with the entire class in order to talk through and reach consensus. This collaboration, as discussed in Chapter 2, facilitated conceptualization. Also, the teacher's presence during the group work and the entire-class discussion allowed her to direct and redirect student discussion as deemed appropriate.

The values in this English lesson and in others taught inductively are many. Stella H. Johnston, an English/Language Arts Coordinator, summarized it this way:

> The values in induction are numerous; some are crucial. For one, learning takes place where it belongs—in the central nervous system. . . . Another is that induction causes teachers and pupils to share common goals, the learning process, and the pleasures of learning. In addition, induction, since it depends on involvement, interaction, and group development of consensus, develops language power. Induction eliminates repetition; you can induce something only once. Any other treatment of the concept is review, drill, or application. Finally, induction trains pupils in patterns of logical thinking—which enables students to find meaning for themselves, a skill and a practice necessary to their growth as thinking, competent adults. (46, p. 7)

Lesson 2. Language Minilesson on Punctuating Dialogue (Grade 8)

This class uses a writers' workshop approach (3). To start the session, the teacher has written a minilesson that deals with quoting and rules for punctuating dialogue. This editing skill is important because conversation is an integral part of the narratives students write.

The teacher begins by having two prompted students come to the front of the classroom and talk to each other about the upcoming class elections. He then asks the class, "How did you know when Tom was talking?" "When Kristen was talking?" Students respond that they could hear them and see their mouths moving.

Next the teacher asks students how writers indicate dialogue since when we read we cannot really hear and see the characters. Students respond that quotation marks are used and statements, such as *Mary said,* indicate which character is speaking.

The teacher then distributes a ditto containing four brief narratives—one an Aesop fable, one a passage from Paul Zindel's adolescent novel, *The Pigman's Legacy,* and two from student writings. All include correctly punctuated dialogue. The teacher instructs students to work with their partners, examine the models, note the punctuation similarities in the dialogue sentences, and write the rules for punctuating dialogue. He points out that some of the dialogue will be split (with the *Mary said* type statement in the middle of one of the sentences of the conversational portion) and some unsplit; therefore, differences between the two types should be noted and rules written for each type. To assist students in including all the pertinent rules for punctuating dialogue, he gives them a visual (shown in Figure 5.2) and tells them to be sure to write one rule that governs each place an arrow appears.

After a few minutes of work time, students report to the entire class and agree on the rules. (For example, "Quotation marks are put at the beginning of what a character says." "Quotation marks are put at the end of what a character says." "If the *said* statement comes after what the character says, a comma, question mark, or exclamation point—not a period—is put before the second pair of quotation marks." "In split dialogue, the second part of a sentence that the character says does not begin with a capital letter unless it is a proper name.")

78

The teacher writes the rules on the board as revisions and agreements are made then students copy the punctuation rules into their notebooks for use when they write narratives.

For immediate practice, the teacher displays two sentences of unpunctuated dialogue on the overhead projector and has students use their rules to punctuate the examples of split and unsplit dialogue. After the correct responses are verified, students are instructed to write two original sentences using the ideas from the conversation of the two classmates who discussed the upcoming class elections at the beginning of the minilesson. They are to write one sentence as unsplit dialogue, and the other as split dialogue.

In this minilesson, students learn a set of principles for punctuating dialogue. They make generalizations that describe relationships between and among concepts (e.g., *quotation marks,*

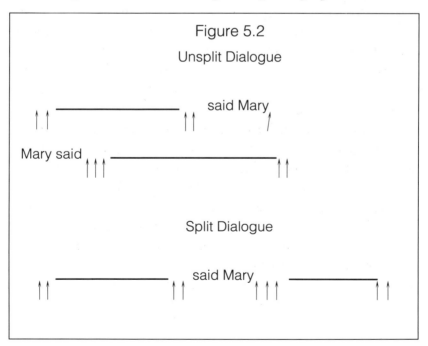

Figure 5.2

Unsplit Dialogue

said Mary

Mary said

Split Dialogue

said Mary

comma, question mark, exclamation point, proper name, split dialogue). The teacher knew that students had knowledge of the prerequisite concepts, and selected interesting examples — student and professional. These included correctly punctuated split and unsplit dialogue using commas, exclamation points, question marks, etc., so that students had specific examples from which to generalize and from which to notice all the components of the generalization.

The teacher's eliciting questions to his students included noting the differences in punctuation for unsplit and split dialogue, the similarities in punctuation for unsplit dialogue, and the similarities in punctuation for split dialogue, in order to generate rules for punctuating dialogue. The visual helped students include all the rules and probably will be an additional reference in the future when they use their rules for punctuating dialogue.

Notice that in this lesson also the students worked collaboratively—first in pairs, then as an entire class to write and revise their class rules for punctuating dialogue. The resulting rules were their language, rather than the teacher's or the often confusing language of the grammar handbook. Thus these rules should be understandable to them when they resurrect them to edit their narratives.

The application activity in this lesson was both immediate and long-term. To verify students' understanding of the principle, the teacher first gave them two unpunctuated sentences to punctuate. Then students applied the principle by creating their own sentences and independently punctuating them. Finally, students will be expected to apply the rules of punctuating dialogue to narratives they write in this writers' workshop class and in other future writing they do. Notice that the teacher did not give a test that has students simply regurgitate the rules learned. Application—correct use—is the goal here.

IDENTIFICATION/ANALYSIS

The following are ideas for three lessons that teachers have used successfully by engaging their students in inductive reasoning in order to learn concepts or principles central to the English discipline. For each description, decide:

1. What is to be learned—a concept or a principle? What is the concept or principle to be learned?
2. What examples are examined?
3. What eliciting questions does the teacher ask, or if they are not provided, what eliciting questions would the teacher most likely ask students?
4. Identify the application activity, or suggest one if one is not provided.

LESSON 1. Have students read several poems by the same writer, whose identity is not revealed. Ask them, "From what we have here, what could you say about this poet?"

> Man? Woman?
> American? British? Other?
> Optimist? Pessimist?
> From the city? Country?
> What ideas and experiences most concern him/her?
> Which poem did he/she write when fairly young?
> Which seems like the work of an older person?

This process is repeated for several poets, in order that students may eventually generalize that a poet's work can provide many clues to his/her life, temperament, etc. (13).

LESSON 2. Students in a tenth grade, Communication Skills and Journalism class do a Children's Literature unit. The teacher introduces the unit by reading to them from children's books for a day. Then students develop criteria for what makes a good children's book. From their criteria, they write their own books for children. They publish their books, including illustrations that they do themselves or they "commission"someone else to do the artwork.

Once the children's books are completed, storytelling is introduced. Students listen to recordings of Bill Cosby, Joe Hayes, and local storytellers, and create their criteria for qualities of good storytelling. Then they practice telling their stories to the class and eventually travel to several elementary schools to read their children's books to younger students (36).

(This lesson description uses the inductive approach twice). Be sure to note the recurrence. Also notice how it employs inductive reasoning for written as well as oral composing.)

LESSON 3. From exposure to 20 of Shakespeare's sonnets, students define Shakespeare's *sonnet* by describing the rhyme and rhythm schemes and the organization pattern as they direct the content. Then students are exposed to five sonnets of Sydney and Spenser and contrast their *sonnet* to Shakespeare's (19).

(Notice that *sonnet* is an example of a concept that has more than one set of essential attributes. Refer to Chapter 3 if you need to review this concept.)

GUIDED PRACTICE

You should now be able to write your own lessons using the inductive approach to teach a concept or a principle. In developing your lessons, use the questions provided in Chapters 3 and 4 to guide you in understanding the nature of the concept or principle to be taught, and in considering the many facets of creating an inductive lesson. If possible, work collaboratively with a partner on your first attempt. Then exchange lessons completed independently with your partner and share critiques. Be sure to give praise—for what is appropriate and should not be changed—as well as changes you think are appropriate or suggestions for alternate ways for different parts of the lessons to unfold.

A. Write an inductive lesson for each of the following objectives:

1. Students will arrive at a class interpretation of a Langston Hughes poem after sharing and debating individual reader response.
2. Students will write a résumé to use in getting a summer job.
3. Students will demonstrate their understanding that "narrative writing is more effective when vivid verbs are used." For example:

"I know who stole the book," *blurted* Mary.

or

"I know who stole the book," *whispered* Mary.

instead of

"I know who stole the book," *said* Mary.

B. Select one unit that is required by your school or district. Identify the fundamental concepts and principles of that unit. Write an inductive lesson for one of the concepts or principles. In your lesson, try to use examples (and possibly nonexamples) in a medium you did not use in the lessons you developed for A above.

Chapter 6

INDUCTIVE REASONING IN MATHEMATICS

> The study of mathematics is one of recognizing patterns and applying them to increasingly abstract sets of numbers, symbols or figures. This phenomenon appears to enhance one's ability to generalize. . . . I seldom, if ever, "tell" students anything because passive learning fails to excite. That would be like leading the horses to water and then shoving their collective head into the trough. (10)

READINESS

The discipline of mathematics provides teachers with opportunities to encourage students to use inductive reasoning in the study of general mathematics, algebra, geometry, consumer mathematics, trigonometry, statistics, etc. The new *Curriculum and Evaluation Standards for School Mathematics* by the National Council of Teachers of Mathematics sets "mathematical power for all" as its goal; one of its standards is students' ability to reason mathematically by using "inductive reasoning to recognize patterns and form conjectures" (25, p. 219). In addition, the *Standards* advocates increased attention to the "active involvement of students in constructing and applying mathematical ideas" and decreased attention to the "teacher and text as exclusive sources of knowledge" (25, p. 129).

To help you apply what you have learned thus far in this book about the inductive approach, specifically to the teaching of mathematics, complete the chart given in Figure 6.1 with concepts and principles fundamental to learning general mathematics, algebra, and geometry. (If possible, share your completed chart with a colleague in the field of mathematics.)

Figure 6.1

	Concept	Principle
General Mathematics		
Algebra		
Geometry		

PURPOSE FOR READING

Following are descriptions of two inductively presented mathematics activities. The first lesson deals with sets, the second with multiplication of integers. As you read, note the following about each lesson:

1. What concept or principle is being learned?
2. What examples are examined by students?
3. What eliciting questions does the teacher ask?
4. What generalization is made?
5. What is the application activity to test student mastery of the concept or principle?

Lesson 1. Pre-Algebra

The teacher begins this class by telling students that today they will be dealing with *sets*. She reminds them that they have used the word "set" through much of their lives when they referred to sets of dishes, sets of tires, etc. Today they will begin to learn about *set* as it relates to mathematics.

Written on the chalkboard is the following information:

Sets	**Not Sets**
A. the Great Lakes	1. large lakes in the world
B. subjects taken this year by all students in this class	2. attractive teachers on this faculty
C. students in this class with red hair	3. good Oriole baseball players
D. whole numbers	
E. students in this class who own a live hippopotamus	

Also, the teacher has set up two displays. The first includes a paint brush, a roller, a bucket of paint, and a box of spackle. This display is labeled *set*. A second display includes a telescope, a piece of cloth, a pack of chewing gum, and a flower. This display is labeled *not a set*.

The teacher then instructs students to examine the *sets* and nonexamples and write down what they believe to be characteristic of a *set*. They are told to consider what the *set* examples have in common and how these examples are different from those labeled *not sets*. After giving students a few minutes for independent thinking, the teacher pairs students to reach consensus on the characteristics of a set.

Next, the teacher leads an entire-class discussion that results in agreement that a *set* is a "clearly defined collection of objects." The teacher tells students that these "objects" are referred to in mathematics as "members" or "elements"; therefore, the generalization becomes "a clearly defined collection of objects, called members or elements." Each nonexample is examined to reinforce understanding that these nonexamples do not possess the critical attribute of a set—that is, they are not "clearly defined" collections because it would be difficult for everyone to agree on what should be in the set. Then the definition of set is recorded in students' notebooks for future reference.

The teacher shows students how to write a set, including

its members between braces and giving the set a capital letter:

A = {   members   }

She explains that this notation is read, "Set A whose members are. . . ."

The teacher then instructs students to designate in this format the examples of *sets* written on the chalkboard. The entire class does the first example as a model:

A = {Lake Michigan, Lake Huron, Lake Erie,
Lake Ontario, Lake Superior}

Pairs of students complete the remaining examples, then the entire class reaches consensus.

B = {Mathematics, English, Social Studies, Science, Foreign Language, Physical Education}
C = {Sara}
D = {0, 1, 2, 3, 4, . . . }
E = {   }

At this point, the teacher introduces the term "empty set" for example E, and the notation for such, ϕ, and asks students to define "empty set." Their definition, "a set that contains no members," is written on the board and copied into their notebooks.

The teacher then asks students if there is a limit to the number of members of a set. She reminds students to reexamine set examples C, D, and E. They conclude that a set may contain from zero to an infinite number of elements. The teacher instructs students to add this information to their essential attributes of a set.

Again working with their partners, students are instructed to write a description for each of the following sets:

A = {a, e, i, o, u, sometimes y}

B = {Saturday, Sunday}
C = {1, 3, 5, 7, 9, . . . }
D = {2, 4, 6, 8, 10, 12, 14, 16, 18}
E = {0, 4, 7, 10, . . . }
F = {0/2, 1/2, 2/2, 3/2, . . . }

Each pair is then grouped with another pair to reach consensus. The teacher circulates to give individual attention to students having difficulty writing the descriptions.

The class concludes with the teacher instructing students to write three mathematics set descriptions and the corresponding listings of members on a separate sheet of paper. One of the descriptions must be for an empty set. Tomorrow the class will begin by having students exchange their descriptions with their partners and complete the listing of members for their partners' descriptions.

In this mathematics class, the concepts *set* and *empty set* are being taught. They are taught in the same lesson because of their interrelationship.

In order to facilitate successful generalization of the attributes of the concepts *set* and *empty set*, the teacher provided simultaneously examples and nonexamples of sets for students to examine. Notice that she moved from sets of general information (the Great Lakes, painting supplies, etc.) to mathematical sets (whole numbers)—that is, from the known and concrete to the unknown and more abstract. She carefully selected examples and nonexamples in order to highlight the essential attributes of *set* and *empty set*. For example, the nonexamples helped students discern the characteristic of "clearly defined" by including a description of members about which there would be controversy as to which objects should be included in a listing of the set. And students learned that a set could be made up of any number of objects, from an infinite number to none, by focusing on

89

example D ("whole numbers") and example E ("people in this class who own a live hippopotamus"), respectively. Also notice that the teacher introduced the mathematical term "member" for the students' word "objects" in their generalization. This was the appropriate time to link new mathematical terminology to what students already knew.

The teacher supplied sets for which students were to write descriptions, but the real application and test to determine if students can independently demonstrate their understanding of the concepts *set* and *empty set* will come when they must write original mathematical set descriptions and listings, including one empty set description.

The interaction in this lesson should not go unnoticed. Initially, students examined the examples and nonexamples of sets alone and tried to formulate their own generalization, then they worked with a partner, and finally with the entire class in order to talk through and reach consensus. This collaboration, as discussed in Chapter 2, facilitated conceptualization. Also, the teacher's presence during the group work and the entire-class discussion allowed her to assist and direct student thinking, and, as deemed appropriate, to help students achieve success.

Lesson 2. General Mathematics

The teacher begins the lesson by telling students they will begin an examination of the multiplication of integers today and by instructing them to complete the table shown in Figure 6.2 and on a transparency.

When students have completed their independent work, the teacher asks for volunteers to record the correct responses on the transparency. Students correctly recorded the products as shown in Figure 6.3.

The teacher asks students:

Examine the numbers multiplied by 5 and describe how they are arranged. (In decreasing order)

90

If this pattern were to continue, what would be the next number to be multiplied by 5? (−1)

So what would be the next factors below 0 × 5? (−1 × 5)

Look at the product column. What happens to each product as the multiplier decreases by one? (Product is 5 less)

Therefore, what would you expect to be the product of −1 × 5 ? (−5)

The teacher instructs students to work with an assigned partner to continue writing the factors and products through the

Figure 6.2		
Factors		Product?
7 × 5	=	
6 × 5	=	
5 × 5	=	
4 × 5	=	
3 × 5	=	
2 × 5	=	
1 × 5	=	
0 × 5	=	

Figure 6.3		
Factors		Product?
7 × 5	=	35
6 × 5	=	30
5 × 5	=	25
4 × 5	=	20
3 × 5	=	15
2 × 5	=	10
1 × 5	=	5
0 × 5	=	0

multiplier –7. He circulates to assist students, and when all have completed their work, he has a student record the components of the table on the transparency (see Figure 6.4).

The teacher asks students to look at the table with positive multipliers of 5, and with their partners to write a rule about the product of two positive integers. The class agrees that the rule is

The product of two positive integers is a positive integer.

or

positive × positive = positive

Then the teacher asks students to examine the table with negative multipliers of 5, and again with their partners to write a rule concerning the product of a negative and a positive integer. The class agrees that the rule is

The product of a negative integer and a positive integer is a negative integer.

or

negative × positive = negative

The teacher asks students for answers to the following problems: 6 × 5   5 × 6

When students respond "30" to both, he asks them to recall what mathematical property makes this so (commutative property for multiplication). Next he asks, "Assuming the commutative property holds for integers, would it make any difference if our tables were written with the negative number as

Figure 6.4		
–1 × 5	=	–5
–2 × 5	=	–10
–3 × 5	=	–15
–4 × 5	=	–20
–5 × 5	=	–25
–6 × 5	=	–30
–7 × 5	=	–35

the second factor in each pair?" (No.) "Then what would be the product of 4 × –5?" (–20)

The teacher reminds students that they know their rules apply when 5 is the constant factor and they begin and end with 7, but they now need to determine if their rules apply to other integers. He assigns each group of four students different integers and instructs them to make a chart like the one they did as a class. When they are ready to defend their decision as to whether the rule holds for their integers, they should raise their hands, and he will listen to their defense.

When all the groups have defended their decisions, the teacher has each group report, revealing that the rules they wrote for multiplication of two positive integers and a positive and negative integer do, indeed, appear to hold for all integers.

As a summary, the teacher distributes the following handout, instructs students to complete the multiplication problems alone, and then verifies the responses with the entire class.

$$-8 \times 4 = \qquad 17 \times -2 = \qquad 12 \times 22 =$$
$$123 \times -13 = \qquad 9 \times 33 = \qquad -87 \times 5 =$$

During the next lesson, the teacher will use the table format again to have students discover the rule for multiplying a negative integer by a negative integer.

In this lesson, two principles of multiplication of integers are taught. Generalizations are made that describe relationships between and among concepts (e.g., *product, negative, positive, integer*). The teacher knew that students had knowledge of these prerequisite concepts because they had previously studied the number line and these concepts had been developed. He was, therefore, able to build on students' knowledge of these concepts and help them discover a principle that related them. Notice that he reviewed a previously learned concept, that of *commutative property*, in the course of the dialogue so that students could apply that concept to their understanding of this principle.

In this lesson, the teacher set up the data in the form of tables so that the pattern was evident to students. His questions (e.g., "Examine the multipliers of 5 and describe how they are arranged in the table.") were deliberately chosen to direct students' attention to the pattern. As a result, they were able to state the desired generalizations, putting them both in formal mathematical terms (e.g., *the product of a negative integer and a positive integer is a negative integer*), as well as more abbreviated terms (e.g., *negative × positive = negative*).

A noteworthy aspect of this lesson is how the teacher built in the opportunity to have several students explain their decision as to whether the principle holds for assigned integers. The group work allowed students to facilitate their learning by talking through their decision, and enabled the teacher to circulate to each group, evaluating and redirecting the learning, if necessary.

The application activity involved students in completing six multiplication-of-integers problems independently. If students had evidenced some difficulty, the teacher might have allowed them to work cooperatively on these. This activity required them to apply the principles they verbalized earlier in the lesson. Additionally, students will build on these principles in a subsequent lesson when the teacher continues with such tables in order to have students generalize that *the product of two negative integers is a positive integer.* If this lesson's strategy has been effective, students should be able to recognize this new pattern even more quickly tomorrow.

In both preceding lessons—set/empty set and multiplication of integers—students are experiencing what the National Council of Teachers of Mathematics is advocating: active involvement in constructing and applying mathematical ideas without the teacher being the exclusive source of knowledge. Thus they are developing "mathematical power": examining, investigating, reasoning, communicating, and developing self-confidence (25, p. 5).

IDENTIFICATION/ANALYSIS

The following are ideas for three lessons that engage students in inductive reasoning in order to learn concepts or principles central to the discipline of mathematics. For each description, decide:

1. What is to be learned—a concept or principle? What is the concept or principle to be learned?
2. What examples are examined?
3. What eliciting questions does the teacher ask, or if they are not provided, what eliciting questions would the teacher most likely ask students?
4. Identify the application activity, or suggest one if one is not provided.

LESSON 1. Give each group of four students a laminated right triangle and a set of one-inch square plastic tiles. Ask students to build squares using each side of the triangle as an edge, and to record the information requested in Figure 6.5.

Show students a larger right triangle that has also had its sides built into squares. This one has been prepared by the teacher and is permanently glued. Have students count the squares used and record the information on a chart as shown in Figure 6.6.

Ask students to look for a pattern among the numbers (number of squares in side c = number of squares in side a + number of squares in side b). Instruct students to reexamine their tile constructions with partners and arrive at a formula for finding side c of a right triangle ($c^2 = a^2 + b^2$). Then introduce the Pythagorean theorem and the work of the Greek scholar Pythagoras.

Give students obtuse and acute triangles and have them

95

attempt the tile procedure and formula application to these triangles. Have students eventually generalize that the Pythagorean theorem only applies to right triangles.

(Notice the use of manipulatives in this lesson. Tiles, rods, unifix cubes, geoboards, and rubber bands, and certain computer programs can help students visualize patterns about which to make generalizations. Also notice that in this lesson, nonexamples [obtuse and acute triangles] are used to limit the generalization derived about finding the length of the third side

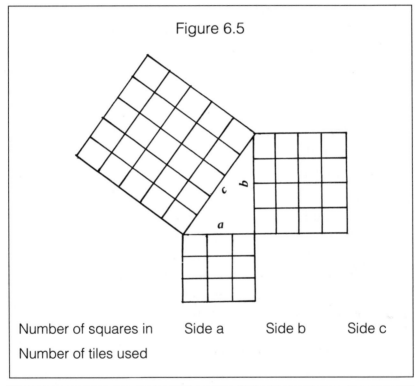

Figure 6.5

Number of squares in	Side a	Side b	Side c
Number of tiles used			

Figure 6.6			
Number of squares in	Side a	Side b	Side c
small triangle	9	16	25
large triangle	36	64	100

of a triangle.)

LESSON 2. Using visuals, review with students the names of the various polygons, and the concepts *vertex, diagonal, adjacent sides,* and *adjacent vertices.* Using the hexagon as an example, and in dialogue with students, draw all the diagonals from one vertex and the remaining diagonals. Next, give students a chart (similar to the one in Figure 6.7) to complete.

Through examination of the chart, lead students to generalize that: (1) the number of diagonals from one vertex is $(n-3)$ where n = the number of sides; and (2) the total number of diagonals = $1/2n(n-3)$ where n = the number of sides. Then instruct students to determine the number of diagonals from one vertex and the total number of diagonals for a dodecagon and a 73-gon (64).

LESSON 3. Have students complete the following exercise by solving for N:

$$5 \times N = 1 \qquad 15 \times N = 1 \qquad 2 \times N = 1$$

Ask students to look at each problem and see if they notice

Polygon	Number of Sides	Number of Vertices	Number of Diagonals from One Vertex	Total Number of Diagonals
Triangle	(3)	(3)	(0)	(0)
Quadrilateral	(4)	(4)	(1)	(2)
Pentagon	(5)	(5)	(2)	(5)
Hexagon	(6)	(6)	(3)	(9)
Septagon	(7)	(7)	(4)	(14)
Octagon	(8)	(8)	(5)	(20)
Nonagon	(9)	(9)	(6)	(27)
Decagon	(10)	(10)	(7)	(35)

Figure 6.7

a pattern within each problem (*N* is the inverted fraction of the first factor). Introduce the term "reciprocal." Have students generate a working definition of "reciprocal," such as "two numbers that have a product of 1."

Instruct students to solve for N in the following and determine if reciprocals hold for fractions.

$$\frac{2}{3} \times N = 1 \qquad \frac{8}{7} \times N = 1 \qquad 4\frac{1}{4} \times N = 1$$

GUIDED PRACTICE

You should now be able to write your own lessons using the inductive approach to teach a concept or a principle. In developing your lessons, use the guidelines provided in Chapters 3 and 4 to help you in understanding the nature of the concept or principle to be taught, and in considering the many facets of creating an inductive lesson. If possible, work collaboratively with a partner on your first attempt. Then exchange lessons completed independently with your partner and share critiques. Be sure to give praise—for what is appropriate and should not be changed—as well as changes you think are appropriate or suggestions for alternative ways for different parts of the lesson to unfold.

A. Write an inductive lesson for each of the following objectives:

1. Students will be able to explain and apply the laws of exponents.
2. Students will be able to explain and apply the distributive property of multiplication over addition.
3. Students will be able to distinguish among the following types of quadrilaterals: rhombus, square, trapezoid, rectangle.

B. Select one unit that is required by your school or

district. Identify the fundamental concepts and principles of that unit. Write an inductive lesson for one of the concepts or principles. In your lesson, try to use examples (and possibly nonexamples) in a medium you did not use in the lessons you developed for A above.

Chapter 7

INDUCTIVE REASONING IN SCIENCE

I attempt to use inductive teaching, but students are so accustomed to memorizing that they protest, "Why don't you just tell us what you want." I suppose we need to do much more with thinking skills, including inductive reasoning. Thinking, observing, classifying—I've seen a serious decline in these skills among students. They have become more passive. They just want to watch, and that frightens me.—Anonymous Teacher

It has taken me 25 years to figure this out, but I have come to the conclusion that good science is the structure of ideas based on observations, and we science teachers ought to be getting that point across with our teaching strategies. Not many textbooks lend themselves well to this approach. (7)

READINESS

Fundamentally, no discipline lends itself to inductive reasoning better or more naturally than science. Experts in the field of science teaching, including a growing number of classroom teachers, acknowledge the inherent relationship between how scientists work and the steps in the inductive process: observing, raising questions, developing generalizations, and applying them to new situations to see if they hold up. Science would appear to be the most convenient and intrinsically sufficient discipline in the curriculum for capitalizing on the curiosity of learners and promoting an inductive view of our world.

In this chapter, we want you to make some useful connections between what you have learned about inductive reasoning in the first four chapters and your skills as a science teacher. As a warm-up for reading the chapter, complete the chart given in Figure 7.1. For each topic fill in a fundamental concept and a fundamental principle. When you have completed the exercise, compare your responses with another science teacher.

PURPOSE FOR READING

How might a biology teacher develop the concept of vertebrates inductively? How might students use a balance beam in a physics class to inductively learn one or more fundamental principles about weights and balance? The two lesson descriptions that follow will take you step-by-step through the inductive process as executed by two teachers. As you follow their lessons, make a written note of the following:

1. What fundamental concept or principle is being learned?
2. What examples are examined by students?
3. What eliciting questions does the teacher ask?
4. What generalization is made?
5. What is the application activity to test student mastery of the concept or principle?

Figure 7.1		
	Concept	Principle
Living Things		
Energy		
The Solar System		

Lesson 1. Vertebrates and Their Characteristics (Grade 9)

The class has completed its study of invertebrates, and the teacher plans to introduce the vertebrates. She has collected still pictures of several examples of these organisms, including pictures of each vertebrate in its natural environment, a diagram of each vertebrate's body plan, and brief descriptions of each vertebrate's behaviors, unique traits, and patterns of interaction with its environment.

On the day she introduces the activity, the teacher explains that the class, having completed its study of invertebrates, is now going to examine another group of living things. She has posted the pictures, body diagrams, and descriptions for each example around the classroom. She organizes the entire class into pairs and instructs each pair to move about the room, pausing to study each example, and together make notes on the similarities among the examples. After 30 minutes she asks students to return to their seats with their notes, join another pair to form groups of four, and compare their lists. Following the small group discussions, she instructs students, still in their groups, to go back to the examples displayed around the room and clear up any items on their lists about which there is lack of agreement in the group. The next day, the groups resume their investigations, examining the displays to verify items on their lists and add any new similarities they discover in the process. She then instructs the groups to be seated and develop a consensus list of similarities common to all examples.

Next, the teacher opens the discussion to the entire class, asking students to name those items on their lists about which their group reached agreement as characteristics of all examples. She writes each suggestion on the chalkboard, asking the class to agree or disagree as she does so. For items on which agreement is not reached, she places a question mark and asks several student volunteers to return to the displays, examine the examples, reach a decision, and report to the class.

At the conclusion of the discussion the class reaches agreement on a list of similarities—that is, the essential attributes of the group of examples. The teacher labels the list on the chalkboard, "Characteristics of Vertebrate Animals," explains that this is the name or label given to animals that share these characteristics, and asks students to copy the list in their logs.

The students are familiar with dissections from their work in previous units of study. The teacher's plan for the next class period will require them, in their groups of four, to dissect a frog and identify whether the frog qualifies as a member of the vertebrate group based on its body plan.

Contrast the approach used by the teacher in this lesson with the approach apparent in many science classrooms: the teacher introduces the topic, assigns students to answer 10 questions on the topic from a chapter in a textbook, gives students an oral or written drill on the content, and asks them to fill out a chart or label parts on a diagram as a summary activity. Does the latter procedure resemble anything like the way in which scientists perform their work? Does it reflect an instructional plan based upon our best knowledge about how learners form concepts?

The teacher in Lesson 1 is teaching the concept *vertebrates* in a manner more consistent with the reasoning applied by scientists in exploring phenomena, and in a way that respects recent knowledge about how learners process new information. She is teaching the concept of vertebrates inductively. She has decided *not* to give students a list of terms to look up or define. Instead, she begins by establishing a purpose for students' learning, and then engages them in research aimed at collecting data by examining pictured examples of the topic. They are looking for patterns—similarities among the examples that might qualify them as members of the same group.

The teacher then helps students analyze the results of their data collecting through the use of directions and eliciting questions, while developing a list of similarities on the chalkboard from their suggestions. Only after students have expressed their findings and reached consensus on the generalizations resulting from their investigations—i.e., the list of similarities—does the teacher introduce the term *vertebrates* as a label for the list of similarities. To test their understanding of the concept, not merely their recognition of the new term, she has students perform a dissection of a frog to see if it qualifies as another example of the vertebrate group.

Most science teachers will recognize the process in the foregoing description as the learning cycle, an inductive teaching strategy originated by the creators of the Science Curriculum Improvement Study, a curriculum project sponsored by the National Science Foundation in the 1960s. The learning cycle consists of three phases. First, students explore new materials and ideas, making observations and collecting notes as they investigate. The teacher acts as facilitator, assisting students by asking questions and providing other prompts. Second, through large-group discussion the teacher leads students to organize their data and look for patterns. She then introduces the vocabulary necessary to label the concept. Third, the teacher introduces a new problem or setting where students can apply the new concept, thereby demonstrating their mastery of the concept.

The learning cycle closely resembles the description of the inductive approach advocated in the first four chapters of this text. Although the learning cycle is organized and described as three phases, it contains the same procedures and rationale essential to the success of inductive reasoning. Like inductive reasoning applied in other content areas, the learning cycle relies on the well-documented principle that understanding a fundamental idea depends on direct experience with appropriate examples of what the idea represents. The approach is inherently more consistent with the thinking and procedures scientists use to develop new ideas and pursue knowledge than are the typical textbook or expository approaches to teaching.

Notice the central role of discussion in this inductive lesson. First, through discussions with a partner, students confirm their initial findings. Then, in groups of four they compare their findings and compile a list of generalizations, in this case a list of similarities. Through questioning, the teacher helps them refine and polish the list. Throughout the discussion process—in pairs, in small groups, and total-class discussions—students are collecting, sequencing, and comparing ideas, developing reasons for their choices, and constructing meanings in their own words—all necessary for the critical thinking and higher-level reasoning skills advocated as priorities for today's secondary classroom. Students in this lesson are not merely memorizing names and labels; they are interpreting data and giving meaning to their experience.

Lesson 2. Balancing (Grade 11)

The teacher explains that the class is going to learn something about balancing. "For instance," he asks, "have you ever wondered how a small child can balance a larger one on a seesaw? It can be done by guessing, or it can be done by understanding and applying a basic principle involved."

He then organizes the class into groups of three and instructs them to work through a series of five exercises. Each group is given a balance, some metal washers (all the same weight), and some paper clips. The written instruction that accompanies each exercise looks like this:

1. Set up your balance with two washers hung at two different places on the left side of the balance center pin. Try balancing this with two washers hung on one paper clip.
2. Change the positions of the washers on the left and repeat the exercise. Try again with only one washer on the left. Make some written notes on your results.

106

3. Does a chain of five washers balance five washers hung from a single paper clip?
4. Will a washer hung at the bottom of a paper clip chain have the same balancing effect as a washer hung at the top of a paper clip chain?
5. Hang two washers from a single paper clip on one side of the balance. Now balance this by hanging two washers on separate clips. Do this several ways and make some notes.

After the groups have completed these five exercises, the teacher asks each group to join another—forming groups of six. Students in each group are to compare their notes on the exercises and come up with some patterns from their data. After a class discussion in which students describe their findings and how they might relate to the seesaw problem, the teacher asks each group to reconvene and come up with a rule, based on their findings, which would permit anyone to complete exercise 5 without guessing.

A few minutes later the teacher asks one group to demonstrate its solution to the class using a balance, and to explain the rule it developed. He writes the rule on the chalkboard. Following some discussion and revisions of the wording of the rule from the discussion, the teacher asks students to accept or reject the rule. They vote to accept.

As an application activity, the teacher gives the class one more exercise using washers and paper clips to solve in their groups. To culminate the lesson, the teacher puts the smallest and largest student in the class on an improvised seesaw and asks the class to balance them using the rule (85).

In this lesson the teacher is using an inductive approach to lead students to a basic understanding about balance. Rather than telling them the principle, requiring them to copy it in their notes and memorize it, and then perform some laboratory activities to "prove" it, he introduces the principle by engaging the students in five firsthand manipulations of materials. Each manipulative activity is problem-centered, stimulating, promotes curiosity, and engages students in observing and reasoning. Note, also, that the five activities require no memorization of terms or definitions as prerequisites to their successful completion.

Then, through a series of directions and eliciting questions, the teacher guides students in arriving at a rule, or principle, that offers an explanation for what they observed, and a systematic, reasoned way of solving balancing problems like those presented in the five activities. Notice, he still has not asked students to memorize a new term or definition; the wording of the principle and its meaning are products of student-generated vocabulary and direct experience, not explanations from a textbook.

Finally, students apply the principle to several additional exercises that require them to demonstrate that they not only recognize, but understand how the principle is applied as a rule for balancing.

As in Lesson 1, you probably recognize here the phases of the learning cycle: exploration of specific examples of the fundamental idea; development of a generalization—in this case a principle—through directions and questioning; and application to a new problem to demonstrate understanding. Specific facts are introduced only when and as they are essential to completing each phase of the inductive process, not as prerequisites to reasoning or firsthand experience. Likewise, vocabulary and definitions are viewed as logical and sometimes necessary outcomes of experience, rather than as determinants of learning in and of themselves.

In this lesson, as in Lesson 1, student interaction is central to the teacher's plan. In each of the five exercises, students are encouraged to collaborate in collecting data, comparing observations, explaining their reasoning, and formulating hypotheses leading to a generalization or principle. The teacher uses well-planned and constructed activities, along with his questions, to guide their interaction. The inductive process is not intended as a casual, do-as-you-please, random discovery approach to formulating ideas; through every step in the process this teacher, like the teacher in Lesson 1, is in charge. The teacher is the architect of the learning environment; the students, however, are the principle architects of the reasoning. Teacher and students share equal responsibility for the outcomes of the experience.

IDENTIFICATION/ANALYSIS

The good news is that a growing number of science teachers are organizing their lessons to promote inductive reasoning, and there is evidence that some text materials are written to present ideas inductively. Three examples of inductively taught lessons for fundamental science concepts or principles follow. For each description, decide:

1. What is to be learned—a concept or a principle? What is the concept or principle to be learned?
2. What specific examples are examined?
3. What eliciting questions does the teacher ask, or if they are not provided, what questions would the teacher most likely ask students?
4. Identify the application activity, or suggest one if one is not provided.

LESSON 1. Have students in pairs make paper airplanes according to a set of specifications for shape and wing size. As they fly the planes, have students keep notes on their performance. "How can you change the plane to fly higher? longer?" "What happens when the wing is made longer? shorter?" "What can you generalize about the features of your plane and its ability to stay aloft?"

Following discussion of the activity and development of

the principle, divide the class into groups of three or four. The challenge to each group is to build and fly a paper plane that will stay aloft longer than that of any other group.

LESSON 2. Students use the microscope to observe the four groups of protozoans—flagellates, ciliates, amoeboids, and sporozoans—on prepared slides. They record distinguishing features of each group, including appearance and movement. (Notice that this is an example of teaching several concepts simultaneously.)

LESSON 3. Have students put a few small rocks and a little pile of sand in a tray of water so that they are partially covered. Pour a few drops of motor oil in the center of the water. Blow on the surface of the water to create currents. "What happens to the rocks and sand?" Dip a small feather in the water, then a few blades of grass or a few small leaves. "What happens?" "What generalizations can you make about the interaction of oil with these elements of the environment?" As a follow up, ask students to study the events of a recent oil spill. What consequences can they predict?

GUIDED PRACTICE

You should now be able to write your own lessons using the inductive approach to teach a concept or principle. In developing your lessons, use the guidelines in Chapters 3 and 4 to assist you in understanding the nature of the concept or principle to be taught, and in considering the many facets of creating an inductive lesson. If possible, work collaboratively with a partner on your first attempt. Then exchange lessons completed independently with your partner and share critiques. Be sure to give praise—for what is appropriate and should not be changed—as well as changes you think are appropriate, and suggestions for alternative ways to structure parts of the lesson.

A. Write an inductive lesson for each of the following objectives:

1. Students will explain why summer is warmer than the other seasons in most areas of the United States. (Astronomy unit)
2. Students will defend classification of the following invertebrates as either *arachnids* or *insecta*: tick and beetle.
3. Students will identify two examples of electrical switches used in their homes and explain how each opens and closes to affect the flow of electrical current.

B. Select one science unit that is required by your school or district. Identify the fundamental concepts and principles of that unit. Write an inductive lesson for one of the concepts or principles. In your lesson, try to use examples (and possibly nonexamples) in a medium you did not use in the lessons you developed in A above.

Chapter 8

INDUCTIVE REASONING
IN SOCIAL STUDIES

I am very stingy about doing students' thinking for them. I do everything within reason to get them to state the generalization themselves. I'll use prompting questions, hints, additional examples, whatever. I will only give the generalization when I am out of time (that is, the end of the class period), or when I absolutely have to move on because I need to accomplish something else to make the lesson a "whole." Having to give the students the generalization is, to me, tantamount to the lesson being unsuccessful. In short, I didn't do it properly. . . . The inductive approach takes time. Thinking takes time. Involvement takes time. Sharing the stage with students takes time, so sometimes I don't "cover" as much as I could by just telling them. That's the rub. But I am willing to make that trade-off. (55)

READINESS

By its very nature, the discipline of social studies is appropriate for the inductive approach because "social studies is a particular way of focusing on patterns of behavior and attitudes" (72, p. 37). These patterns translate into concepts and principles in the specific disciplines of history, geography, economics, sociology, anthropology, psychology, political science, and related fields.

To help you integrate what you have learned about inductive reasoning in the first four chapters ot this book with your skills as a social studies teacher, complete the chart given in Figure 8.1. For each area of social studies named, fill in one or more fundamental concepts and principles. If possible, share your completed chart with another social studies teacher.

PURPOSE FOR READING

Descriptions of two inductively presented social studies lessons follow. The first is an introductory civics lesson designed to motivate students who will take a state-required citizenship test. The second is a geography lesson focusing on the geographer's use of maps. As you read, note the following for each lesson:

1. What concept or principle is being learned?
2. What examples are examined by the students?
3. What eliciting questions does the teacher ask?
4. What generalization is made?
5. What application activity is used to test student mastery of the concept or principle?

Lesson 1. *Characteristics of Citizenship (Grade 8)*

The teacher begins the class by asking students to write for five minutes in response to the question, "In your opinion, what is a 'good citizen'?" When students have completed their own reflective writing, the teacher puts them into groups of four and asks them to compare what they have written in response to the question. He encourages them to clarify any questions they may

Figure 8.1

	Concept	Principle
History		
Geography		
Economics		

114

have of another student's response in order to ensure understanding of the views of each member of their group.

Next, the teacher distributes a handout containing a series of quotations from famous individuals stating their ideas about "a good citizen." The handout includes several quotes, including the following:

> Amongst the virtues of the good citizen are fortitude and patience. William Cobbett, 1829

> The first requisite of a good citizen in this republic of ours is that he shall be able and willing to pull his weight. Theodore Roosevelt, 1902

> Political activity is the highest responsibility of a citizen. John F. Kennedy, 1960

> A good citizen is one who doesn't always keep his mouth shut. Anonymous

The teacher instructs students to discuss each quote, first by translating it to be sure they understand it, and then by attempting to reach consensus on whether they agree or disagree with the individual's point of view.

After adequate time for discussion, the teacher instructs students in each group to identify the characteristics of the "good citizen" they all agree on, and to write their own operational definition of the concept. The teacher informs students that minority reports will be accepted if the group is unable to reach consensus.

After several minutes of group deliberation, the teacher leads an entire-class discussion, first asking each group reporter to share those characteristics of a "good citizen" on which the group was able to agree. A master list of characteristics on which the entire class agrees is ultimately completed after debates, justifications, and deliberations. At this time, the teacher is also eligible to express his opinions.

For homework, students are given the assignment of

testing the reality of their list by interviewing an adult; the purpose of the interview is to find out if the person interviewed fulfills the characteristics of a good citizen as delineated by the class. Students will have an opportunity to report the results of the interviews during the next class period. The teacher reminds them that the identity of the adult should remain anonymous.

In this lesson, students learn the concept of *a good citizen.* It is a concept in that "good citizens" share common characteristics—essential attributes. This concept, however, does not lend itself to an absolute list of attributes; therefore, the teacher encouraged students to debate the issue and even encouraged minority reports. Although the teacher in his planning no doubt arrived at his own list of essential attributes, he set up this lesson in such a way that he was willing to accept the consensus of the class members.

Notice that the teacher had students examine three sets of examples—operational definitions—of the "good citizen." First, they reflected on their own beliefs through writing, then they compared their ideas with those of their peers, and finally they read and interpreted the thoughts of famous individuals on the topic in order to affirm and/or broaden their original beliefs.

In order to arrive at a generalization, the teacher instructed students to list the characteristics of a good citizen on which all group members agreed. In essence, students were told to identify the pattern of similarities.

The application activity in this lesson required students to test their concept of citizenship by using the list to interview an adult (parent, relative, friend, another teacher).

The peer interaction in this lesson should be noted. By working in small groups and then with the entire class, students were provided opportunities to learn by talking the problem through with others—to test the validity of their initial ideas and to reshape them if appropriate.

Lesson 2. Population Densities (Grade 11)

Throughout the year, the social studies teacher has emphasized the ways maps are used by geographers to study how people have arranged and organized their living space. Today she announces to the class that they are going to examine some physical environmental factors that influence where people live. Giving students world maps showing population densities, she asks them to describe what they see on the map and interpret what it might mean. Through discussion, students describe the location of major population clusters on the map.

"Would you describe the distribution of population as very even and systematic throughout the world, or uneven?" asks the teacher. "What geographic factors might account for these patterns of population distribution?" Following this brief discussion aimed at tapping students' information background on the topic and arousing their curiosity, she tells them she would like them to examine a collection of world maps to see if they can find a pattern of relationships between the world's physical features, on the one hand, and the distribution of the world's population, on the other.

The teacher organizes the class into small groups and distributes a package of four physical feature world maps to each group: soil productivity, rivers, rainfall, and elevation. She asks the groups to examine the four maps in the package, along with the map of population distribution, and find physical features that correspond to population clusters. They are to use the continent of North America as the site of their first investigation.

After the groups have had time to examine the maps and discuss their findings, the teacher asks each group to give a brief report, identifying the major population clusters in North America and the physical features that appear to be related to them. She develops a list of relevant physical features on the chalkboard from the group reports. Students discuss the list, refer to their maps to verify their findings, and reach consensus on the following generalization: population clusters occur in areas of low relief, on or near fertile soils, and proximate to waterways.

Having used North America as a first example, the teacher then instructs the class to focus on a second continent, Asia, examining the maps, and deciding in their groups whether the generalization they have agreed to holds up. Following the groups' examination of Asia, and class discussion, students review the stated generalization to see if it can be accepted as a general principle to explain how population distribution and geographic features are related.

As a final step, the teacher assigns each group a different continent and instructs them to use the principle to see if they can explain the distribution of population on that continent. For homework, students are to draw on a large sheet of newsprint an imaginary continent, showing some examples of the four physical features and placing at least three population clusters on the continent, and be able to explain why the latter would be located where they are in terms of the continent's physical features.

This lesson focused on a fundamental geographic principle about the relationship of the earth's physical features and population distribution. The lesson depended on the teacher's ability to successfully integrate several essential geographic concepts: population clusters, elevation, and soil productivity, along with basic knowledge about rivers and rainfall. Her purpose was to lead students to a principled understanding of the forceful influence the landscape exerts on people's choices about how and where they live. Using the inductive approach, she (1) introduced the topic; (2) permitted students to explore selected materials—maps, which were relevant to the topic; (3) provided a class setting where students could organize and discuss their findings; (4) used eliciting questions and other prompts to lead them to a generalization; and (5) instructed them to apply their understanding of the generalization by creating a map of their own.

And look at the consequences: the teacher can be confident that students can not only use a map to locate population densities, but that they also understand and can explain how the land's physical features influence where people live. As an approach to developing this fundamental geographic principle, consider how much more likely the goal is achieved this way, that is, inductively, than by asking students to simply locate 10 major population clusters on a world map and make a list of them, or by giving students the generalization and then pointing out several examples on a wall map.

In using the inductive approach, the teacher is also reinforcing some basic reasoning skills used by geographers as well as other researchers: how to locate and classify information, how to interpret findings, and how to report results. None of these skills would be required of the students in this lesson if the teacher relied on an expository approach, even though they might come up with the "right answers" on a test requiring them to locate or recall 10 major population clusters.

A primary and necessary consideration of the teacher, therefore, is what he or she values as the primary outcome of learning the content of the social studies discipline. Mere recall of specific information is a very probable result of expository teaching; inductive teaching, on the other hand, places the responsibility for reasoning—not just remembering—where it belongs, with the learners, not the teacher. It invites students to think and reason as a social scientist—that is, combing through examples, sorting through content, developing hypotheses about cause and effect, reaching conclusions, and making applications.

Student interaction is a central feature of the approach used in this lesson. Students are interacting to collect information from their maps, comparing ideas, sorting out what is relevant to the topic and what is not, discussing the reasons for their choices, and defending their opinions against those of other students in their group. Well-planned student interaction, therefore, can be justified on more than the social or pedagogical pretext of providing variety in classroom activities (i.e., an option to the lecture and seatwork); it can be posed as a necessary intellectual means for clarifying ideas as part of the reasoning process.

IDENTIFICATION/ANALYSIS

The following are ideas for three inductive lessons that teachers have used successfully to teach concepts or principles central to the social studies discipline. For each lesson description, decide:

1. What is to be learned—a concept or a principle?
2. What examples are examined?
3. What eliciting questions does the teacher ask, or if they are not provided, what eliciting questions would the teacher most likely ask students?
4. What application activity is used? (If one is not mentioned, suggest one.)

LESSON 1. Students examine world maps showing the location of major earthquakes. The teacher poses the questions: "What do you suppose causes earthquakes?" "Why do major ones tend to occur where they do?" Students then study a world map showing the location of the earth's plates and the principal locations of plate tectonics. "What relationships do you see between the location of major earthquakes and the pattern of plate tectonics?" asks the teacher. Through a follow-up series of eliciting questions, further comparisons between the two maps, the teacher leads the class to state a principle about the relationship between plate tectonics and earthquakes.

LESSON 2. Students are instructed to collect from magazines and newspapers a series of advertisements that they consider to be effective. In class, students examine their ads and those of their peers, and generalize various appeals advertisers use (39).

LESSON 3. The teacher displays many pictures showing primitive and advanced technology. The pictures include obvious examples of each—for example, a woman beating a rug and a modern vacuum cleaning system, a boy fishing with a pointed spear and a fisherman with hip boots, vest, hat, and modern rod and reel. Students are instructed to examine each picture carefully. When a student is ready, he or she places one picture next to the "primitive" sign or next to the "advanced" sign. The teacher tells the student if the placement is correct. This process continues until all the pictures are correctly placed.

The teacher instructs students to examine the examples and the nonexamples of advanced technology and to formulate a definition of the term "technology" (37).

GUIDED PRACTICE

You should now be able to write your own lessons using the inductive approach to teach a concept or a principle. In developing your lessons, use the guidelines in Chapters 3 and 4 to guide you in understanding the nature of the concept or principle to be taught, and in considering the many facets of creating an inductive lesson. If possible, work collaboratively with a partner on your first attempt. Then exchange lessons completed independently with your partner and share critiques. Be sure to give praise—for what is appropriate and should not be changed in the lesson—as well as changes you believe should be made, and suggestions for alternative ways to develop the lesson.

A. Write an inductive lesson for each of the following objectives:

1. Students will be able to explain "imperialism" and decide if this is an appropriate descriptor for the United States' role in Latin America (20).

121

2. After determining the causes of the 1920 depression, students will decide if the United States is heading toward another depression.
3. Students should be able to defend their own political leanings as either liberal, moderate, or conservative.

B. Select one social studies unit that is required by your school or district. Identify the essential concepts and principles of that unit. Remember, we have urged that inductive teaching be used primarily to teach concepts and principles fundamental to the discipline, not routine information or masses of data. Write an inductive lesson for one of the concepts or principles. In your lesson, try to use examples (and possibly nonexamples) in a medium you did not use in the lessons you developed for A above.

BIBLIOGRAPHY

1. Amidon, Edmund, and Flanders, Ned A. "The Effects of Direct and Indirect Teacher Influence on Dependent-Prone Students Learning Geometry." *Journal of Educational Psychology* 52, no. 6 (December 1961): 286–91.

2. Askin, Carol. In "National Survey: Inductive Teaching in English." Unpublished survey data collected by Gloria A. Neubert and James B. Binko, 1989.

3. Atwell, Nancie. *In the Middle: Writing, Reading, and Learning with Adolescents.* Upper Montclair, N.J.: Boynton/Cook, 1987.

4. Ausubel, David P. *The Psychology of Meaningful Verbal Learning.* New York: Grune and Stratton, 1963.

5. Babikian, Yeghia. "An Empirical Investigation to Determine the Relative Effectiveness of Discovery, Laboratory, and Expository Methods of Teaching Science Concepts." *Journal of Research in Science Teaching* 8, no. 3 (November 1971): 201–9.

6. Barnes, Douglas. *From Communication to Curriculum.* New York: Penguin Books, 1984.

7. Beach, John E. In "National Survey: Inductive Teaching in Science." Unpublished survey data collected by Gloria A. Neubert and James B. Binko, 1989.

8. Begle, E. G., ed. *Mathematics Education.* Chicago: University of Chicago Press, 1970.

9. Binko, James B., and Neubert, Gloria A. "Inductive Reasoning: A Model for Infusion in Teacher Education." *Thinking and Teacher Education* 1, no. 1 (February 1990): 5–7.

10. Booth, Penelope. In "National Survey: Inductive Teaching in Mathematics." Unpublished survey data collected by Gloria A. Neubert and James B. Binko, 1989.

11. Boyer, Ernest L. *High School: A Report on Secondary Education in America.* New York: Harper and Row, 1983.

12. Breaux, Robert. "Effects of Induction Versus Deduction and Discovery Versus Utilization of Transfer of Information." *Journal of Educational Psychology* 67, no. 6 (December 1975): 828–32.

13. Brewbaker, James M. In "National Survey: Inductive Teaching in English." Unpublished survey data collected by Gloria A. Neubert and James B. Binko, 1989.

14. Bruffee, Kenneth A. "Collaborative Learning and the 'Conversations of

Mankind.'" *College English* 46, no. 7 (November 1984): 635–52.

15. Bruner, Jerome S. *Toward a Theory of Instruction.* New York: W. W. Norton, 1966.

16. Bruner, Jerome S.; Goodnow, Jacqueline J.; and Austin, George A. *A Study of Thinking.* New York: John Wiley and Sons, 1967.

17. Butler, Tom. In "National Survey: Inductive Teaching in Science." Unpublished survey data collected by Gloria A. Neubert and James B. Binko, 1989.

18. Carnine, Douglas. "New Research on the Brain: Implications for Instruction." *Phi Delta Kappan* 71, no. 5 (January 1990): 372–77.

19. Cline, Ralph M. In "National Survey: Inductive Teaching in English." Unpublished survey data collected by Gloria A. Neubert and James B. Binko, 1989.

20. Coombs, C. Garn. In "National Survey: Inductive Teaching in Social Studies." Unpublished survey data collected by Gloria A. Neubert and James B. Binko, 1989.

21. Cooper, James M., ed. *Classroom Teaching Skills.* 3d ed. Lexington, Mass.: D. C. Heath, 1986.

22. Craig, Robert C. *The Transfer Value of Guided Learning.* New York: Teachers College Press, 1953.

23. ____. "Directed Versus Independent Discovery of Established Relations." *Journal of Educational Psychology* 47, no. 4 (April 1956): 223–34.

24. *Crossroads in American Education.* A report of the National Assessment of Educational Progress. Princeton, N.J.: Educational Testing Service, 1989.

25. *Curriculum and Evaluation Standards for School Mathematics.* Reston, Va.: National Council of Teachers of Mathematics, 1989.

26. Davis, Robert B. "Discovery in the Teaching of Mathematics." In *Learning by Discovery: A Critical Appraisal,* edited by Lee S. Shulman and Evan R. Keislar. Chicago: Rand McNally, 1966.

27. DeRobbio, Barbara B. In "National Survey: Inductive Teaching in Social Studies." Unpublished survey data collected by Gloria A. Neubert and James B. Binko, 1989.

28. Egelston, Judy. "Inductive Versus Traditional Methods of Teaching High School Biology Laboratory Experiments." *Science Education* 57, no. 4 (October–December 1973): 467–77.

29. *Essentials of English.* Urbana, Ill.: National Council of Teachers of English, 1982.

30. Fraivillig, Judith L. In "National Survey: Inductive Teaching in

Science." Unpublished survey data collected by Gloria A. Neubert and James B. Binko, 1989.

31. Gagne, Robert M. *The Conditions of Learning.* New York: Holt, Rinehart and Winston, 1965.

32. ____. "Varieties of Learning and the Concept of Discovery." In *Learning by Discovery: A Critical Appraisal,* edited by Lee S. Shulman and Evan R. Keislar. Chicago: Rand McNally, 1966.

33. ____. "The Learning of Concepts." In *Instructional Design: Readings,* edited by M. D. Merrill. Englewood Cliffs, N.J.: Prentice-Hall, 1971.

34. Gagne, Robert M., and Smith, Ernest C., Jr. "A Study of the Effects of Verbalization on Problem Solving." *Journal of Experimental Psychology* 63, no. 1 (January 1962): 12–18.

35. Goodlad, John I. *A Place Called School.* New York: McGraw-Hill, 1983.

36. Graff, Pat. In "National Survey: Inductive Teaching in English." Unpublished survey data collected by Gloria A. Neubert and James B. Binko, 1989.

37. Harris, Judy J. In "National Survey: Inductive Teaching in Social Studies." Unpublished survey data collected by Gloria A. Neubert and James B. Binko, 1989.

38. Heiman, Marcia; Narode, Ronald; Slomianko, Joshua; and Lochhead, Jack. *Teaching Thinking Skills: Mathematics.* Washington, D.C.: National Education Association, 1987.

39. Hennies, Mary Lea. In "National Survey: Inductive Teaching in Social Studies." Unpublished survey data collected by Gloria A. Neubert and James B. Binko, 1989.

40. Hermann, G. D. "Learning by Discovery: A Critical Review of Studies." *Journal of Experimental Education* 38, no. 1 (Fall 1969): 58–72.

41. ____. "Egrule Versus Ruleg Teaching Methods: Grade, Intelligence, and Category of Learning." *Journal of Experimental Education* 39, no. 3 (Spring 1971): 22–42.

42. Hermann, G. D. and Hincksman, N. G. "Inductive Versus Deductive Approaches in Teaching a Lesson in Chemistry." *Journal of Research in Science Teaching* 15, no. 1 (January 1978): 37–42.

43. Horak, Virginia M., and Horak, Willis J. "The Influence of Student Locus of Control and Teaching Methods on Mathematics Achievement." *Journal of Experimental Education* 51, no. 1 (Fall 1982): 18–21.

44. Hovland, Carl I., and Weiss, Walter. "Transmission of Information Concerning Concepts Through Positive and Negative Instances." *Journal of Experimental Psychology* 45, no. 3 (March 1953): 175–82.

45. Hull, C. L. "Quantitative Aspects of the Evolution of Concepts." *Psychological Monographs* 28, no. 1 (1920): Whole no. 123.

46. Johnston, Stella H. "Why Teach Inductively?" Baltimore: Baltimore County Public Schools, September 24, 1970. (Photocopy.)

47. Joyce, Bruce, and Weil, Marsha. *Models of Teaching.* Englewood Cliffs, N.J.: Prentice-Hall, 1980.

48. Kagan, Jerome. "Learning, Attention and the Issue of Discovery." In *Learning by Discovery: A Critical Appraisal,* edited by Lee S. Shulman and Evan R. Keislar. Chicago: Rand McNally, 1966.

49. Kersh, Bert Y., and Wittrock, Merlin C. "Learning by Discovery: An Interpretation of Recent Research." *Journal of Teacher Education* 13, no. 4 (December 1962): 461–68.

50. Klausmeier, Herbert J. *Educational Psychology,* 5th ed. New York: Harper and Row, 1985.

51. Koran, John J.; Koran, Mary Lou; and Freeman, Patricia. "Acquisition of a Concept: Effects of Mode of Instruction and Length of Exposure to Biology Examples." *AV Communication Review* 24, no. 4 (Winter 1976): 357–66.

52. Kreiger, Elliot. "Shakespearean Crossroads: Teaching Shakespeare Through Induction." *College English* 39, no. 3 (November 1977): 286–89.

53. Kurfiss, Joanne G. *Critical Thinking: Theory, Research, Practice, and Possibilities.* ASHE-ERIC Higher Education Report No. 2. Washington, D.C.: Association for the Study of Higher Education, 1988.

54. Laird, Charlton Grant. *The Miracle of Language.* Cleveland, Ohio: World Publishing, 1953.

55. Lawlor, James C. In "National Survey: Inductive Teaching in Social Studies." Unpublished survey data collected by Gloria A. Neubert and James B. Binko, 1989.

56. Levine, Daniel U. "Teaching Thinking and Other Higher-Order Skills to Low Achievers." *Houghton Mifflin's Educators' Forum* (Fall 1988): 1.

57. Lott, Gerald W. "The Effect of Inquiry Teaching and Advance Organizers upon Student Outcomes in Science Education." *Journal of Research in Science Teaching* 20, no. 5 (May 1983): 437–51.

58. MacEwan, Barbara. In "National Survey: Inductive Teaching in Social Studies." Unpublished survey data collected by Gloria A. Neubert and James B. Binko, 1989.

59. McTighe, Jay. "The Need to Improve Student Thinking: A Rationale Statement." Baltimore: Maryland State Department of Education, n.d. (Photocopy.)

60. Mager, Robert F. *Preparing Instructional Objectives.* Rev. ed. Belmont, Calif.: David S. Lake Publishers, 1984.

61. Makarovich, Michal. In "National Survey: Inductive Teaching in English." Unpublished survey data collected by Gloria A. Neubert and James B. Binko, 1989.

62. Marzano, Robert J.; Brandt, Ronald S.; Hughes, Carolyn Sue; Jones, Beau Fly; Presseisen, Barbara Z.; Rankin, Stuart C.; and Suhor, Charles. *Dimensions of Thinking: A Framework for Curriculum and Instruction.* Alexandria, Va.: Association for Supervision and Curriculum Development, 1988.

63. Montague, Earl J. *Fundamentals of Secondary Classroom Instruction.* Columbus, Ohio: Merrill, 1987.

64. Murray, Brenda. In "National Survey: Inductive Teaching in Mathematics." Unpublished survey data collected by Gloria A. Neubert and James B. Binko, 1989.

65. Narode, Ronald; Heiman, Marcia; Lochhead, Jack; and Slomianko, Joshua. *Teaching Thinking Skills: Science.* Washington, D.C.: National Education Association, 1987.

66. National Commission on Excellence in Education. *A Nation At Risk: The Imperative for Education.* Washington, D.C.: U.S. Department of Education, 1983.

67. Neilsen, Allan R. *Critical Thinking and Reading: Empowering Learners to Think and Act.* Monograph on Teaching Critical Thinking, no. 2. Bloomington, Ind.: ERIC Clearinghouse on Reading and Communication Skills, and Urbana, Ill.: National Council of Teachers of English, 1989.

68. Parker, Walter C. "Teaching Thinking: The Pervasive Approach." *Journal of Teacher Education* 38, no. 3 (May–June 1987): 50–56.

69. Presseisen, Barbara Z. *Thinking Skills: Research and Practice.* Washington, D.C.: National Education Association, 1986.

70. Renner, John W.; Abraham, Michael R.; and Birnie, Howard H. "Secondary School Students' Beliefs About the Physics Laboratory." *Science Education* 69, no. 5 (October 1985): 649–63.

71. Resnick, Lauren B. *Education and Learning to Think.* Washington, D.C.: National Academy Press, 1987.

72. Rosenblum-Cale, Karen. *Teaching Thinking Skills: Social Studies.* Washington, D.C.: National Education Association, 1987.

73. Shulman, Lee S., and Keislar, Evan R., eds. *Learning by Discovery: A Critical Appraisal.* Chicago: Rand McNally, 1966.

74. Sieger-Ehrenberg, Sydelle. "Concept Development." In *Developing Minds: A Resource Book for Teaching Thinking,* edited by Arthur L. Costa.

Alexandria, Va.: Association for Supervision and Curriculum Development, 1985.

75. Sigel, Irving E. "A Constructivist Perspective for Teaching." *Educational Leadership* 42, no. 3 (November 1984): 18–21.

76. Sizer, Theodore R. *Horace's Compromise: The Dilemma of the American High School.* Boston: Houghton Mifflin, 1984.

77. Smith, Frank. "The Politics of Ignorance." In *Essays Into Literacy*, edited by Frank Smith. Portsmouth, N.H.: Heinemann, 1983.

78. ____. *Insult to Intelligence.* Portsmouth, N.H.: Heinemann, 1986.

79. Taba, Hilda; Durkin, Mary C.; Fraenkel, Jack R.; and McNaughton, Anthony H. *A Teacher's Handbook to Elementary Social Studies.* Reading, Mass.: Addison-Wesley, 1971.

80. Taba, Hilda, and Elkins, Deborah. *Teaching Strategies for the Disadvantaged.* Chicago: Rand McNally, 1966.

81. Tama, M. Carol. "Critical Thinking: Promoting It in the Classroom." *Digest.* Bloomington, Ind.: ERIC Clearinghouse on Reading and Communication Skills, June 1989.

82. Tennyson, Robert D., and Park, Ok-Choon. "The Teaching of Concepts: A Review of Instructional Design Research Literature." *Review of Educational Research* 50, no. 1 (Spring 1980): 55–70.

83. Vygotsky, Lev S. *Mind in Society: The Development of Higher Psychological Processes.* Cambridge, Mass.: Harvard University Press, 1978.

84. Weimer, Richard C. "An Analysis of Discovery." *Educational Technology* 15, no. 9 (September 1975): 45–48.

85. Wessner, John, and Ukens, Leon. *Activities in Physical Science: A Nontext.* Dubuque, Iowa: Kendall/Hunt Publishing Co., 1988.

86. Wright, David P. "Interactions Between Instructional Methods and Styles of Concept Learning." *Journal of Educational Research* 70, no. 3 (January–February 1977): 150–56.

87. Yeany, Russell, Jr. "A Case from the Research for Training Science Teachers in the Use of Inductive/Indirect Teaching Strategies." *Science Education* 59, no. 4 (October–December 1975): 521–29.

88. Zaslavsky, Orit, and Movshovitz-Hadar, N. "Editorial—Independent Learning of College Mathematics: An Inductive Approach." *UMAP Journal* 7, no. 4 (Winter 1986): 277–80.

89. ____. "Inductive Problem-Sequences for Independent Study of Linear Algebra." *Journal of Mathematics and Science Technology* 19, no. 3 (November 1988): 421–34.

90. Zerphey, Robert G. In "National Survey: Inductive Teaching in Social Studies." Unpublished survey data collected by Gloria A. Neubert and James B. Binko, 1989.